LEBANESE COOKING

AN INTRODUCTION TO THIS SPECIAL MIDDLE EASTERN CUISINE

LEBANESE COOKING

AN INTRODUCTION TO THIS SPECIAL MIDDLE EASTERN CUISINE

SUSAN WARD

Quantum Books

A QUANTUM BOOK

Published by
Quantum Publishing Ltd.
6 Blundell Street
London N7 9BH

This edition printed 2003

ISBN 1-86160-617-6

QUMLEB

Printed in Singapore by
Star Standard Industries (Pte) Ltd

CONTENTS

INTRODUCTION

A COUNTRY AND A CUISINE

My Lebanon . . . was a cloak of many colors. Beirut was Levantine to the heart, astute, multilingual, many-minded and with an element of sheer bawdy wickedness. Tripoli up north . . . was Sunni, fanatic, austere. Tyre and Sidon slept in the sand by the sea. The people of the plain were not the people of the mountain, a mile away.

Thus wrote Albion Ross, American journalist and *aficionado* of Lebanon, in 1957, when the troubles that would eventually overtake it were first erupting. Both recurrent civil war and the escalation of the Arab-Israeli conflict have devastated what was once the pride of the eatern Mediterranean – a democracy on a nation of minorities, all living in a golden-green land half the size of Wales. Of course, that "cloak of many colours" was sewn with faulty thread. The seams came undone, and the fabled tolerance of the artificial nation carved from Syria by the French Mandate of 1860–6, and made independent in 1946, was shown to be based on a myth the populace itself could no longer afford to believe.

The sun rises over fishing boats in the harbour at Tyre.

A farmer in the Bekkah Valley ploughs using traditional methods.

This brief introduction to the tragedy that has overtaken one of the most beautiful, productive and culturally fascinating parts of the Middle East may seem out of place in a cookery book. However, to ignore the divisions that have brought it about is also to misunderstand the diversity and richness of Lebanon's heritage, reflected in the diversity and richness of its table. Lebanon has played host to invaders, refugees, settlers and merchants since 2000 BC; today it claims to be the only country in the world whose population is composed entirely of minorities, though all call themselves Arabs. These divisions, drawn along religious lines, are reflected in the influences that have united to create Lebanese cuisine.

The large Muslim population is divided almost equally between Sunnis and Shiites, the latter group augmented in the past 20 years by many Palestinian refugees. The two groups have traditionally been almost as suspicious of one another as of non-believers. The very slightly smaller Christian population is dominated by the Maronites, an ancient sect, united to Rome since the thirteenth century. The Maronites, by virtue of their commercial success and historical ties with France, have long been the most educated, cosmopolitan group in the country, and have actively cultivated the sophistication associated with all things French. It is largely a result of their powerful influence that the French tongue is almost as widely heard as Arabic, the official language; a triumph of their business acumen that Beirut became the "Paris of the Middle East". To the honeypot of Beirut came foreign adventurers, investors, tourists and twentieth-century settlers from Europe; it is an indication of the city's pre-civil war international bias that masses at Beirut's two major Roman Catholic churches were held not only in French and Arabic, but also in English, Italian, German, Spanish and, occasionally, Polish.

The other important minorities include the Druse, a secretive religious sect whose feats of arms are legendary; Orthodox and Catholic Greeks; Armenians and Syrians; and a small community of Jews.

It is the Arabic-Muslim tradition that has ensured the survival of herbed or spiced olive oil and lemon juice as the ubiquitous dressing and marinade; that has confirmed the domination of yoghurt over cream (a French contribution); that accounts for the prevalence of lamb-based meat dishes and the absence of pork; that has developed the range of *meze* to triumphant heights, and has incorporated a variety of nuts into savoury dishes and made them one of the mainstay of sweets, pastries and such rare delicacies as green almond jelly.

It is the French-Maronite influence that has brought wine to the table and vinegar into the kitchen; that has introduced new and succulent vegetables into cultivation and the Syrian truffle into fine Beirut restaurants; that has refined the sometimes agressive spicing of the East into a subtlety appreciated by Westerners. These two main traditions have historically welcomed the contributions of neighbours and the other ethnic communities: the dates of the Iraqis and the dried fruit dishes of the Jews and Palestinians; the beef dishes and meat stews of the Armenians; the pomegranate seeds and sumac of the Iranians and Syrians; the pasta of the Italians.

Before the war, Lebanon was the richest agricultural region in the Eastern Mediterranean after Israel. Topographically, it is a kind of mini-California. A warm coastal plain, cultivated with citrus fruit and bananas, gives way to foothills covered in vineyards and orchards of apricots, plums and peaches; soil-poor outcrops provide adequate subsistence for olive and fig trees, goats and sheep. The rains falling on the high mountains behind feed the agrarian paradise of the Bekkah Valley, nestled between the first mountain range and the second, larger barrier straddling the eastern border with Syria.

The River Litani, its tributaries and canals, are responsible for the richness of the Bekkah, truly a "land of milk and honey". Here grow the plumpest fruits and vegetables, and here graze the fattest livestock; the vines looking down on the valley grow on the rootstock brought by the Jesuits almost 200 years ago.

Along the rocky banks of the Bardoni, an offshoot of the Litani, lies the resort of Zahle. In better times, tourists and the inhabitants of Beirut and the coast would flock to its rustic cafés and outdoor restaurants on the weekends, to eat *mezze,* drink coffee, wine and *arak,* and smoke the traditional *narghileh,* or water pipe. Today, the tables are largely empty – former patrons now more concerned with survival than good living. In Beirut itself, the hotels are vacant; the swimming pools, dry holes. The curtain has rung down on the famous Casino du Liban, 25 km/16 miles up the coast – on its floorshows, gambling, restaurant complex and theatre. Only the people whose lives are tied to the country remain.

But optimism is the lifeblood of the Lebanese people, and there are signs that it is flowing with renewed energy. A solution to the Arab-Israeli conflict would mean another chance for a viable Lebanese state, whatever compromises might have to be made between interest groups. Already Lebanese government tourist offices are back in operation, though as yet they have little to promote in their home country. That, we hope, is to come; meanwhile the delights and seductions of Lebanese cooking are becoming more widely known through restaurants, delicatessens and even supermarkets in the West. If we can share in the gustatory pleasures of the country now, how much more eager will we be to sample them in the sunny Mediterranean land from which they come?

LEBANESE EATING – IN AND OUT

Farmers and shepherds are hard at work soon after sunrise; shops and offices are usually open by 8.30 am. This is the lightest meal of the day, consisting typically of *labneh* (yoghurt cheese) with *khoubz* (Arab bread). Olives, dates, fresh fruits, honey and nuts will also share the table. Country people may eat a bowl of *ful medames* (small brown fava beans), while eggs, fried or hard-boiled, are another alternative.

Lunch, taken between 1 pm and 3 pm, can be the main meal among rural folk, but more usually it is an abbreviated spread of *meze* with fresh *khoubz.* In Beirut and other large towns, snack bars have proliferated, as they have in Western cities; they are life-savers for the office worker.

Dinner, for most Lebanese, is the main meal of the day, taken with the whole family. Eaten between 8 pm and 11 pm, it consists of a selection of *meze* – the number and quality of which are dictated by the occasion and the prosperity of the family – grilled meat or poultry (or, on the coast, fish), accompanied by burghul – the usual grain – or less frequently, by rice.

Among Beirut's middle classes, and throughout Lebanon's large Christian communities, the segregation common in the rest of the Arab world between men and women at meals is not customary. Lebanese women are seen eating (and drinking) in restaurants, and they entertain mixed company in their homes.

In Beirut before the troubles, every type of international restaurant drew Lebanese citizens and tourists. Today, the restaurant scene has disintegrated, but the expertise and experience are there to be resurrected when better times return.

Of the Lebanese Arab-style restaurants (*mat'am*) and cafés, some specialize. There are restaurants serving charcoal-grilled lamb dishes (*mat'am lahem mashwi*) and fish and seafood (*mat'am samak*); there are non-alcoholic snack bars serving *shawarma* (*mah'em asir*), patisseries (*helaewayat shami*) and cafés offering *mezze* and *arak* (*kas arak wi mezze*).

Snow melts in the mountains above a village and terraced fields.

TREASURES OF THE LEBANESE DELICATESSEN

Most Middle-Eastern delicatessens in Britain and the United States have a preponderance of either Lebanese-produced or Lebanese-style staples and prepared foods on their shelves. This is partly because of the traditional role of the Lebanese as businessmen/importers, and partly because of the especially high regard in which the Lebanese refinements of the Arab table are held. The varied influences that have shaped the country have also given the food a cosmopolitan appeal, in both preparation and presentation. Although many of the same dishes are found in neighbouring Syria and Jordan – and even, with a slightly different accent, in Egypt or Turkey – much of what we Westerners today appreciate as "Middle-Eastern" cuisine has, somewhere along the way, been edited and elevated by Lebanese taste and polish.

Imagine that you have entered a typical Middle-Eastern food shop. On narrow wire racks you may find a range of dried spices and herbs, some prepacked by large firms, others in hand-labelled plastic bags produced by members of a small family business. On rows of shelves are displayed a selection of largely unfamiliar dried or tinned pulses and grains – beans in shades of brown, white and red; green, brown or red lentils; and packets and boxes of burghul, semolina (North African couscous and Levantine *moghrabieh*), and Egyptian and Syrian *fariek* (whole wheat). Farther along are bottles of olive oil, rose and orange flower waters, and syrups, in slight variations by a myriad of producers, for cooks are noted for devotion to their favourite brands.

There will be more shelves – or perhaps a central island – piled with fresh fruits, vegetables and selected herbs. Many of the vegetables are ones less frequently encountered in this country, such as fresh shelled broad beans (*ful akdar*); okra (*bamia*); small, pale green, pear-shaped courgettes (*kousa*), baby purple or striped aubergines (*bazinjan*) and fresh green olives for home pickling. In trays, or packaged in bags will be dried fruits – figs (*tihn*), dates (*tamar* or *bayleh*), apricots (*mishmish*) – as well as nuts and dried seeds (*mohamahsat*). The Arab love of nuts has been developed to an obsession in Lebanon; in addition to the usual plain unsalted varieties for cooking – in Lebanon mainly pistachios (*fosto*), pine nuts (*sonoba*), almonds (*lohz*), cashews and, to a lesser extent, walnuts (*en'gamael*) – there will always be a selection specially prepared for nibbling: lemon-flavoured or salted pistachios, or pistachios encased whole in a kind of sweet brittle cake (*fosto illieh*); two or three kinds of salted almonds (*lohz*); cashews and peanuts (*ful sudani*). The melon seeds on offer make a popular snack; while sesame seeds (*sum sum*) – either plain or toasted – appear in everything from *tahini* to breads and desserts.

Dominating the delicatessen will probably be two or three cold cabinets. Those hidden at the back of the shop contain regional cheeses and homemade yoghurt, prepared spiced minced meat for kebabs, and a selection of *mezze* and salads: *sambousek* and *fatayeer* (savoury pastries stuffed with meat, spinach or cheese); deep-fried *kibbeh bi shamiyeh* (ground lamb and burghul cases stuffed with a lamb and pine nut mixture), *houmus* and *tabbouleh* (cracked wheat salad). Ranged along the counter are jars of oil-pickled cheeses (*shanklish*); below, great earthenware bowls hold black or green olives, some awash in marinades ripe with whole chillies and lemon slices, others in pools as black as pitch.

In the glass case facing the street will be the jewels of the collection, a mouth-watering display of small sweet pastries, most with a dusting of bright green, ground pistachio. They draw the eyes of passers-by, tempting them into this gastronomic Aladdin's cave. The selection may include varieties of *mam'oul*, sweet-dough balls and ovals filled with chopped dates, pistachios or walnuts; crisp phyllo-covered pastries like *asabieh* – cigar-shaped "fingers" filled with chopped cashews – or *bohaj*, "packets" enfolding pistachio or mixed nuts. Pride of place is ceded to the internationally renowned *baklava* – diamond-shaped slices sticky

A vegetable barrow in a Beirut market.

with perfumed syrup, whose typical Lebanese filling is pistachio or cashew (rather than the walnuts common in Turkey and Greece).

To lovers of Middle-Eastern food – whether by birthright or conversion – crossing the threshold of a shop such as this is never simply "shopping". Like the French, the Levantine peoples take great interest in their food; they live to eat, rather than eat to live. Deciding upon purchases necessitates discussion of quality and debate upon methods and recipes – spiced with gossip or an exchange of family news. As in the "old country", food shops act as centres for the community – perhaps even more so in a Western metropolis, where links with tradition are harder for people to maintain.

As for the Western initiate, the elements of epicureanism, fascination and curiosity are inextricably combined. There is always something new to appreciate – a packet never noticed before, a different-shaped pastry to try, a taste to experience. It takes a spirit of adventure of course – to ask, to buy and, ultimately, to try – but the rewards far exceed the effort.

A-Z OF INGREDIENTS AND SPECIALITIES

The following ingredients and staples are those that are typically Middle-Eastern, with particular emphasis on items characteristic of Lebanon. They will be found in most good delicatessens and/or Middle-Eastern shops. I have used the Arabic name (in approximate phonetic English) as the identifying term when it is the one by which a dish or ingredient is commonly known, even among Westerners.

Arak: a spirit distilled from grape juice and flavoured with aniseed. Similar to Greek *ouzo,* it is somewhat lighter in flavour and less syrupy in consistency.

Basturma: a cured and smoked fillet of beef, dark red in the centre and covered with a thick coating of spice. It is a variation of Israeli *pastourma* and a predecessor of the better-known Armenian *pastrami.*

Beans: the most popular include light-brown broad beans (*ful nabed*) and the small, darker brown *ful medames,* with their characteristic black "eye". The latter are a much beloved staple of everyday life, eaten as a snack, at breakfast and in main dishes. Other common varieties include white haricot beans (*ful baladi sa'ideh*) and fresh green beans (*loubieh*), which are served as a *mezze*/salad, accompaniment or stewed with meat. (See also *houmus,* below)

Green beans in olive oil.

Burghul: wheat grain that has been lightly cooked, dried and ground, either to a fine or medium-coarse grade. It is available unhusked (wholewheat) or, more commonly, husked (bleached). Fine-ground burghul is used for making *kibbeh* and *tabbouleh;* the medium-coarse for stuffings and stews such as *imjadra.*

Bread: the undifferentiated Arabic term *koubhz* – "bread" – is used for very different types of this staple, from the common flat individual round, to wholewheat sheets, to the sesame-covered versions. In rural areas it is baked by the family in earthen ovens; in towns and villages it is the province of the baker. Bread is eaten in great quantities throughout all meals.

Cheeses: Lebanese cheeses are usually very white, made from the milk of goats or sheep. The most common is *labneh,* homemade or available prepared, which is a condensed yoghurt used both as a dip and in cooking. *Shanklish* are little balls of *labneh,* coated in mint, thyme or other herbs, and bottled or served covered in oil. *Anari,* a sheep's milk cheese, is available both wet – as a kind of ricotta – and dry for grating. *Gibeh beideh* is a salty white cheese similar to Greek Fetta, which is usually substituted for it abroad. *Kallaje,* and the more familiar Turkish *halloumi,* are sharper, maturer cheeses with a rather rubbery texture, often served fried with bread or eggs. Syrian *gibneh jaduleh* ("braided cheese") has the appearance its name implies. It has much the same consistency as mozzarella and is used in the same way.

Lebanese bread.

Coffee and Tea: *gowhwa* (coffee) and *shay* (tea) are both consumed in great quantities, though coffee is undoubtedly the king of Lebanese drinks, with its "prime time" after dinner. Both beverages are served in small, handleless cups – tea often in glasses. Unlike Turkish coffee, the Lebanese version is decanted into a pot before serving, so it does not possess the heavy sediment associated with much Middle-Eastern-styled coffee. The coffee and sugar are brewed together, so that the diner must let his host or waiter know whether he wishes his coffee very sweet (*sokah ziyaday*), medium (*mazbout*) or without sugar (*sayeday*). Lebanese coffee is traditionally flavoured with ground cardamom (which can be added to the freshly ground coffee when you buy it from a shop). (Less frequently, cinnamon – which is supposed to be an aphrodisiac – is substituted for the cardamom.) After several cups of coffee following the meal, Lebanese diners then move on to several cups of tea.

Both tea and coffee are also enjoyed anytime during the day, and cafés are full of men (though in Lebanon women, too, frequent restaurants and cafés) smoking the water pipe (*nargileh*) and passing the time of day. Tea is served sweet, but less so than the North African version, and the mint leaves typically added to Arab tea are not left to stew. Rather they are added to the pot – or the glass itself – just before the tea is served.

Flower waters: orange flower water and rosewater are used in desserts and sweets, notably in *mam'oul* and phyllo-wrapped pastries. Orange flower water is also boiled with water to produce Lebanese "white coffee", a digestive appreciated after meals.

Houmus garnished with paprika and parsley.

Houmus: the term is used both for the whole chickpeas and for the creamy paste made from the ground pulses and seasoned with lemon juice, olive oil, garlic, herbs and spices (page 36). It is served as a *mezze,* but also accompanies grilled dishes such as chicken, shish kebab or *shawarma* (q.v.).

Kishik: a dehydrated wheat and yoghurt product, used more in Iranian cookery, but which has certain limited uses in the Lebanese kitchen. Available in packets and in bottles, it must be reconstituted with water before being used in dips and to make *Manakeish bi Za'atar* (pizza-like dough topped with *kishik,* thyme and olive oil, a variation of *Lahem bi Ajine,* page 44).

Malbalm: long, brownish-pink sticks with a waxen appearance made from grape juice boiled down to a gum-like consistency and mixed with nuts. It is a sweetmeat sold on the streets and in shops from Turkey to Egypt, though that available in Western delicatessens usually comes from Cyprus.

Moghrabieh: tiny semolina balls sold dried in packets, used to thicken Lebanese chicken soup. It is not an ingredient you will encounter in restaurants or at Lebanese-style dinner parties – it is a peasant dish, like the rustic soups thickened with tapioca pearls in parts of Western Europe.

Nuts: the most popular Lebanese nuts are pistachios (*fosto*) and pine nuts (*sonoba*); both are used across the range of cooking, from *mezze* to sweetmeats and desserts. To a lesser degree, almonds (*lohz*), cashews (*kaju*) and walnuts (*en'gamael*) make an appearance.

Sweet spiced pistachios.

Oils: the other major cooking agent used by Lebanese cooks, in addition to *samneh* (q.v.), is olive oil. Since olives themselves are treated with such imagination and pickled in so many ways, it is not surprising that olive oil holds a valued place in the kitchen. Less flavoursome oils – vegetable and sunflower – have made few inroads into Lebanese cooking. A traditional cooking fat, *alyeh,* obtained from exceptionally fattened sheep (particularly from the tail) was once popular in the mountain and desert regions of the Levant, but is much less used today.

Phyllo: a pastry made from flour, water and oil originally developed in ancient Greece. It is rolled extremely fine to an almost paper-thin consistency, and is used for both sweet and savoury pastries, including *sambousek* and *baklava.* Difficult to make at home, except for a cook experienced in its preparation, phyllo is available in commercial packets composed of large sheets.

Pomegranate seeds: although the seeds are used primarily in Iranian and Syrian cooking, they make their appearance in some Lebanese stuffings and salads, providing a piquant, slightly sour-sweet taste.

Samneh: this is simply clarified butter. In Lebanon it has a distinctive flavour, since it is usually made from sheep's (or less commonly, goat's) milk. When made from cow's milk, it is the same as Indian *gee,* which still has a stronger taste than ordinary butter. It was developed before the days of refrigeration, and its long cooking and subsequent refinement from impurities means that it will keep for several months and can withstand higher temperatures than ordinary butter. However, in most cases where a traditional recipe calls for *samneh,* ordinary butter or a mixture of butter and oil will be adequate, though lacking *samneh*'s pungent undertones.

Sausages: Levantine sausages are usually made from lamb or beef, and are made to be grilled over a fire. They include *makaneh,* and the very spicy dried *sujuk,* sometimes cut into pieces and mixed with *batatas harras* (Fried Potatoes, page 101) or other vegetable dishes which a cook wants to "lift".

Shawarma: a large conical hunk of sliced raw lamb and fat, compressed around a vertical split. This stands before a special gas or electric fire, which grills the meat as it rotates, basting itself. The thin slices cut off as the outer layers of the meat cooks are stuffed into Arab bread pockets, together with onions and a spicy sauce. Special equipment is needed both to make the compressed *shawarma* and to cook it, so it is served in special snack bars or street stalls. It is a close relative of Turkish döner kebab.

Tahini: a paste made from ground toasted sesame seeds emulsified with olive oil, lemon juice and garlic. This basic staple of Lebanese and Arabic cuisine can be made at home, but is often bought prepared in bottles (preferable to the tinned variety). It is used to make dips and other dishes, but can also be used on its own as a dip.

Vine leaves: in Lebanon vines grow abundantly around doorways and over verandahs, so that fresh young leaves are always available. Abroad, they must often be bought in plastic packets or tinned, and preserved in brine. They must be soaked and drained before they are used.

Wine and **Beer:** the Bekkah Valley is the centre of Lebanese wine growing; the first vines were planted by Jesuit missionaries in 1857. They are still in production, despite the war. The best vineyards are Château Musar, a heavy dark red, and the rosés, Château Kefraya and Domaine des Tourelles.

The best-known Lebanese brands of beer are Almaza and Laziza.

Yoghurt: in Lebanon, yoghurt is usually made from sheep's or goat's whole milk, and is a much richer, thicker product than we are used to in the West. It is used in salads, main courses and desserts; drained and condensed it becomes *labneh,* which is a form of creamy sour cheese.

Cucumber and yoghurt salad.

THE LEBANESE HERB GARDEN

**Denotes the herbs most frequently used.*

Coriander

***Coriander** (*kuzbarak*): although it looks very much like flat-leaved parsley, this herb has a more acrid taste which makes it suitable for all types of savoury cooked dishes, salads and *mezze.*

Dill (*shabeth*): a dry-climate, feathery member of the umbellifer family, which is good when used as a flavouring for fish and salads.

Marjoram

Wild Marjoram (*rigani*): the wild variety is preferred to the cultivated in Lebanon; it imparts a distinctive peppery flavour to marinades for kebabs and to a few casseroles. Wild marjoram does not grow in Britain or the United States.

***Mint** (*na'na*): spearmint and peppermint grow abundantly throughout the Middle East and are the two varieties of the large mint family used in cooking. Mint is added fresh to tea, salads and meat dishes, marrying particularly well with cucumber and lamb. Donkeys bearing great panniers overflowing with mint cuttings clip-clop down highways from Morocco to Turkey.

Mustard and Cress (*barbe'en*): a sharp-flavoured salad ingredient and garnish, recognizable from its tiny double leaves topping each stem.

***Parsley** (*bagdunish*): parsley used in the Middle East is always flat-leaved with, some maintain, a slightly stronger flavour than the curly variety.

Sage

Sage (*maraniyeh*): used in marinades for kebabs, roasted meats and stuffings. It has a dominating taste which should be treated with care.

Thyme

Thyme (*za'atar*): makes an appearance in stuffings and stews, though not with the frequency it does in the western Mediterranean.

THE LEBANESE SPICE CABINET

**Denotes the spices most frequently used.*

Allspice

***Allspice** (*bahar hahilu*): perhaps the premier spice in Lebanese cookery. The small round berries of the Jamaican pepper tree seem to encapsulate the flavours of cloves, cinnamon and nutmeg, though allspice has no relation to any of them. Since these three spices are much appreciated in Lebanon, allspice is often used in dishes where they might otherwise appear, or in combination with them for added impact.

Aniseed (*yansoun*): the flavouring used in making *arak* (see the A-Z earlier), aniseed is also used in savoury dishes and sweets.

Black cherry kernel (*mahlab*): this uniquely Arabic spice is made from the pale brown kernel found inside the stone of the black cherry. Sold whole, it must be ground to a powder. Although it is used mainly in Syrian and Iranian cooking, it appears occasionally in Lebanese pastries and breads.

Black pepper (*filfil aswad*): used as much in Arabic as in Western cooking.

Caraway (*karawayeh*): the seeds of this relative of aniseed and fennel are used in salads and savouries; occasionally in Arab pastries.

Caraway

***Cardamom** (*hab'han*): fresh green cardamom pods are used in savoury dishes, though less than in India. The back seeds are ground to flavour coffee (q.v.).

***Cinnamon** (*kirfy*): cinnamon, the inner bark of trees found in Sri Lanka, shaved into quills, was an important trade commodity to the Levant long before the Crusades. It appears in a large number of Lebanese dishes, flavouring the spectrum of dishes from *mezze* to pastries and desserts.

Chilli (*bisbas*): fresh thin green chillies are found in the basket of vegetables presented at the beginning of a Lebanese meal; beware, they are fiery! Green chillies and dry red chillies also appear in several savoury dishes, though not as frequently as they do in North African cuisine.

Cloves

Cloves (*kabsh kurnful*): like cinnamon, these hardened flower buds have long been an important part of Lebanese cuisine, both sweet and savoury.

Cumin (*kammun*): less popular than in North Africa, cumin nevertheless is grown locally and used in salads, meat dishes and marinades.

Lebanese spice mix: this does not have a standard name in Arabic, nor is there a standard recipe; it is devised by each cook to taste. It is made ahead of time, in order for the flavours to mingle, and used when required. A guideline proportion might be 4 parts ground cinnamon, 1 part ground cloves, 1 part ground chilli, 1 part green cardamom pods.

Nutmeg (*jawajz a'tib*): the ground or grated nut appears in sweet or savoury dishes, although allspice (q.v.) is more commonly used.

Paprika (*filfil hilu*): this spice is not widely exploited in Lebanon. It is used mostly as a garnish.

Saffron (*za'faran*): sparingly used in Lebanese cooking, primarily as a colouring for rice. It does not receive the respect it gets in Iranian and Indian cooking.

Sumac (*sumac*): this is a spice made from the crushed berries of the sumac tree. It is used primarily in Iranian cooking, but appears in Lebanese *Fatayeer* (page 41) and is occasionally used as a condiment like pepper, to be sprinkled over salads and savoury dishes. It is an acquired taste, having a bitter flavour.

Turmeric (*kurkum*): like saffron, this is used infrequently and sparingly as a colourant for rice dishes. Its flavour is bitter and its colour more garish than that of saffron.

Turmeric.

SUGGESTED MENUS

A SUMMER LUNCH PARTY

Chilled Artichoke Soup

◆

Sardine-stuffed Lemons (*Hamid Mashi wi Saerdin*)
Stuffed Vine Leaves (*Warah Inab*)

◆

Beef and Barley Salad
Ful Medames

◆

Orange Yoghurt Cake

A HOT AND COLD VEGETARIAN PARTY

Cheese Balls (*Shanklish*)
Lebanese Avocado Dip (*Avocado bi Tahini*)
with Arab Bread (*Khoubz*) or Pitta
Beirut Olives

◆

Chickpea Balls (*Falafel*)
Savoury *Baklava*
Lebanese Bread Salad (*Fattoush*)

◆

Vegetable Layer (*Mousakha'a*)
Lentils and Burghul (*Imjadra*)

◆

Orange Sorbet
Pine Nut Macaroons

A FISH-LOVER'S DINNER

Spinach and Yoghurt Soup (*Labenaya*)

◆

Clams or Mussels Marinière, Tyre-style

◆

Baked Stuffed Fish (*Samak Harrah*)
Potatoes with Chickpeas (*Batatas bi Houmus*)

◆

Grapefruit and Avocado Salad

◆

Nut-stuffed Flaky Pastry (*Baklava*)

A CLASSIC LEBANESE SPREAD FOR TEN

Hot Mixed Crushed Nuts (*Muhamara*)
Chickpea and *Tahini* Dip (*Houmus bi Tahini*)
Aubergine Dip (*Moutabel*)
Yoghurt Cheese Dip (*Labneh*)
All with Arab Bread (*Khoubz*) or pitta

◆

Cooked Stuffed Minced Lamb Balls (*Kibbeh bi Shamiyeh*)
Cooked Cheese on Bread (*Kallaje*)
Grilled Sardines (*Saerdin Mashwi*)
Pickled Vegetables (*Kabbis*)

◆

Cracked Wheat Salad (*Tabbouleh*)
Sweet-Sour Aubergine (*Bazinjan Rahib*)

◆

Lebanese Shish Kebab (*Lahem Mashwi*)
Garlic Chicken Wings (*Jawaneh*)
Pilau Rice

◆

Yoghurt with Honey and Almonds

A SIMPLE FAMILY MEAL

Lebanese Spring Vegetable Soup

◆

Stewed Lamb and Okra (*Bamia Maslu*)
Lentils and Rice (*Mudardara*)

◆

Semolina Cake (*Basboosa*)
Cinnamon Ice Cream

A STAND-UP DRINKS PARTY

Spiced Almonds (*Lohz*)
Dried Apricot and Cheese Mounds
Stuffed Bekkah Radishes
Deep-fried Almond Squid
Spiced Fruit Meatballs with Mint Yoghurt Dip
Little Spinach Packets (*Fatayeer*)
Stuffed Fish Balls (*Kibbeh Samak*)
Small Courgette Puffs (*Aggah bi Kousa*)

SOUPS
SHURBA

CHILLED ARTICHOKE SOUP

SERVES 6

The thistle-like artichoke grows well in the sandier, poorer soils outside the main vegetable-producing Bekkah Valley. In Lebanon, whole small artichokes would be used, but frozen – or even a good brand of tinned – artichoke bottoms will do in countries with less profusion!

- *1.15 l/2 pints chicken stock*
- *10–12 frozen or tinned artichoke bottoms in brine, drained and coarsely chopped*
- *90 ml/3 fl oz whipping cream*
- *20 ml/4 tsp lemon juice*
- *Salt and freshly ground pepper*
- *Cayenne pepper*
- *1 small red pepper, cored, seeded and finely chopped*
- *8 spring onions, white parts only, finely chopped*

In a large saucepan, combine the stock and the chopped frozen or tinned artichokes. Bring to a boil, reduce heat, cover and simmer for about 10 minutes. Remove from the heat and purée in batches in a blender or food processor fitted with a metal blade. Rub the purée through a strainer into a large bowl and allow to cool somewhat. Stir in the cream and lemon juice; add salt, pepper and cayenne to taste. Cover and chill overnight.

Before serving, taste the soup and adjust seasoning, if necessary. Divide the soup among 6 bowls and serve, garnished with a sprinkling of red pepper and spring onion.

LENTIL SOUP WITH GARLIC AND ONION

SHURIT 'AADS

SERVES 6–8

Lentils are a staple of Lebanese peasant cooking – and of Middle-Eastern cuisine in general. For soups the small red variety are the most often used, since they soften quickly and have a slightly less earthy flavour than other varieties.

- *450 g/1 lb red lentils, washed and drained*
- *2.25 l/4 pints beef or lamb stock*
- *2 large onions, chopped*
- *2 celery stalks, chopped*
- *1 large beef tomato, peeled, seeded and chopped*
- *30 ml/2 tbsp* samneh
- *Salt and freshly ground pepper*
- *7.5 ml/1½ tsp ground cumin*
- *20 ml/1½ tbsp* Taratoor bi Sade *(page 111)*
- *Lemon quarters*

In a large saucepan, bring the stock to the boil. Add the lentils, half the onions, the celery and tomato. Bring back to the boil, lower the heat, cover and simmer for about 50 minutes.

Meanwhile, in a small frying pan, melt half the *samneh* over a medium heat. Add the remaining onions and sauté gently, stirring continuously, until the onions are soft and caramelized. Take the pan off the heat and reserve.

When the lentils and vegetables are soft, purée the soup in batches in a blender or food processor fitted with a metal blade. Return the soup to the saucepan, add salt and pepper to taste, the cumin, and the *Taratoor*. Reheat for about 5 minutes, stirring. Just before serving, stir in the remaining *samneh*.

Ladle into bowls and garnish each with some of the caramelized onions. Serve with lemon quarters to squeeze into the soup.

CUCUMBER AND CUMIN SOUP

SERVES 6

Perfect for a hot day, this is a Levantine version of a soup popular throughout the Middle East, Turkey and the Balkans.

- *2.5 ml/½ tsp cumin seed*
- *4 cucumbers (about 450 g/1 lb), peeled, seeded and chopped*
- *2 small garlic cloves, minced*
- *250 ml/8 fl oz buttermilk*
- *Salt and freshly ground pepper*
- *6 thin slices lemon*

Spread the cumin seeds on a baking tray, and toast gently under a grill until lightly coloured. Turn the cumin seeds, chopped cucumbers, garlic and buttermilk into a blender or food processor fitted with a metal blade and process until smooth.

Pour the soup into a large bowl, season to taste, and chill for several hours. Serve the soup in bowls, with a thin slice of lemon floating on the top.

SPINACH AND YOGHURT SOUP

LABENAYA

SERVES 6

Popular in Egypt, Jordan and Lebanon, this soup is more usually made with beet greens, which impart a characteristic, slightly sour, flavour. When the more easily obtainable spinach is used, as in this recipe, a touch of light white wine vinegar will help to approximate the taste.

- *1 garlic clove, minced*
- *475 g/16 fl oz Greek-style yoghurt*
- *Large pinch turmeric*
- *45 ml/3 tbsp olive oil*
- *1 large onion, finely chopped*
- *450 g/1 lb spinach leaves, washed thoroughly and shredded*
- *2 small leeks, finely chopped*
- *100 g/4 oz long-grained rice*
- *1.15 l/2 pints vegetable stock*
- *45 ml/3 tbsp white wine vinegar (champagne vinegar, if available)*
- *Salt and freshly ground pepper*

In a bowl, whisk together the garlic, yoghurt and turmeric. Set aside to let the flavours mingle.

Heat the olive oil in a large casserole and stir in the onion. Sauté until lightly coloured and softened, then stir in the spinach, leeks and rice. When the spinach has wilted and the rice is coated, pour the vegetable stock and the vinegar. Season to taste. Bring to the boil, then reduce the heat, cover and simmer for about 15–20 minutes, until the rice is tender.

Just before serving, take the soup off the heat. Whisk in the yoghurt mixture, and then ladle immediately into bowls.

LEMON CHICKEN SOUP

SERVES 6

Chickens in the peasant areas are very much free range and, since they are valued for their eggs, can live to a ripe age (for a chicken!). Older hens find their way into soups like this one.

- *3–4 lb free-range chicken, cut into pieces*
- *750 ml/1¼ pints chicken stock*
- *1 medium onion, chopped*
- *2 large beef tomatoes, peeled, seeded and chopped*
- *1 tbsp fresh tarragon leaves*
- *1 tsp grated lemon peel*
- *Salt and freshly ground pepper*
- *2 Cyprus potatoes, peeled and chopped*
- *225 g/8 oz okra, topped and tailed*
- *50 g/2 oz canned chopped jalapeño chillies*
- *100 g/4 oz frozen sweetcorn kernels*
- *Juice of 1 lemon*
- *Chopped flat-leaved parsley*
- *Paprika*

In a large casserole, combine the chicken pieces (except for the breasts), the stock, onion, tomatoes, tarragon and peel. Pour over 3 cups of water, season to taste, and bring to the boil. Reduce the heat, cover and simmer for 20 minutes. Add the breasts and continue to cook until the breasts are just cooked through. Remove all the chicken pieces from the soup with a slotted spoon and set them aside to cool.

Add the potatoes to the soup, cover and continue to simmer until the potatoes are done, about 25 minutes; add the okra after 10 minutes.

When the chicken is cool enough to handle, remove the meat from the bones, discarding the skin. Chop the meat into small pieces. Add to the soup, together with the chillies and corn kernels. Bring the soup back to the boil, reduce heat, and simmer for 5 more minutes. Stir in the lemon juice and serve immediately, garnished with chopped parsley and paprika to taste.

LEBANESE SPRING VEGETABLE SOUP

SERVES 6

When the fresh spring vegetables come into season – particularly the prized fava bean – they find their way into soups like this one, a version which has been influenced by the Sephardic Jews who have passed through Lebanon.

- *1.15 l/2 pints chicken stock*
- *1 Spanish onion, finely chopped*
- *2 small garlic cloves, minced*
- *2 stalks celery, finely chopped*
- *Salt and freshly ground pepper*
- *2 leeks, topped, cleaned and thinly sliced into strips*
- *5 artichoke hearts, chopped*
- *275 g/10 oz shelled fava beans (or broad beans, if unavailable)*
- *60 ml/4 tbsp finely chopped mint*
- *60 ml/4 tbsp finely chopped coriander*
- *60 ml/4 tbsp finely chopped flat-leaved parsley*
- *Cayenne pepper*
- *Pitta bread, split in half lengthwise, toasted and torn into shreds*

In a large saucepan, combine the chicken stock, onion, garlic cloves, celery and seasoning to taste. Add 350 ml/12 fl oz of water to the pan. Bring the mixture to the boil, then reduce the heat and simmer for about 15 minutes. Add the leeks, artichoke hearts, and fava beans, and simmer for 35 minutes or until the beans are tender. Take off the heat, and stir in the fresh herbs and cayenne to taste.

Allow the herbs to infuse in the soup for a few minutes, then serve with the shredded, toasted pitta scattered over the top.

TOMATO AND CORIANDER SOUP

SERVES 6

Coriander is a familiar herb in Lebanese dishes, to which it imparts a tang far more appealing than its rather foetid smell would suggest. This is a summer soup, using the lush tomatoes of the inland valleys, and would make an excellent preliminary to a fish or poultry main dish.

- *1.5 kg/3 lb ripe, plump tomatoes, roughly chopped*
- *175 ml/6 fl oz tomato juice*
- *3 tbsp freshly squeezed orange juice*
- *1 Greek or Italian pickled pepper, seeded*
- *4 ml/¾ tsp caster sugar*
- *Ice water*
- *60 ml/4 tbsp finely chopped fresh coriander*
- *150 ml/¼ pint Greek-style yoghurt*

In a blender or food processor fitted with a metal blade, purée the tomatoes, onion and orange juices, pepper and sugar until it is as smooth as possible. Press the purée through a sieve, rubbing with a wooden spoon to force as much through as possible. Discard the residue, and add enough ice water to thin the purée to a soup-like consistency. Stir in the coriander, cover and chill until cold. Pass the yoghurt separately at the table, to allow guests to add as much of it as they wish.

Lebanese Spring Vegetable Soup.

SIDON MELON SOUP

SHURBAT SHAEMAN

SERVES 6

Melons of all types – green, yellow and orange – grow profusely on the small farms of the inland valleys and, until the Middle East crisis, were among the prime exports of the country. When at their peak, they are pleasing simply cut in half or quarters. This ingenious two-tone soup can make use of slightly over-ripe fruit.

- *2 large ogen or honeydew melons, peeled, seeded and chopped*
- *60 ml/4 tbsp lime juice*
- *60 ml/4 tbsp caster sugar*
- *2 large cantaloupe melons, peeled, seeded and chopped*
- *60 ml/4 tbsp lemon juice*
- *120 ml/4 fl oz Greek-style yoghurt*
- *Ground cinnamon*
- *Mint leaves*

In the bowl of a blender or food processor fitted with a steel blade, purée the ogen melon, lime juice and 30 ml/2 tbsp sugar until smooth. Pour into a pitcher, cover and chill until cold.

Rinse out the bowl of the processor or blender and fill with the cantaloupe melon, lemon juice and remaining sugar. Purée until smooth. Pour into a pitcher, cover and chill until cold.

When ready to serve, position each soup bowl in front of you. Pick up both pitchers, and pour the two soups into the bowl at the same time, one on each side. Repeat with the remaining bowls.

Each soup will be two-tone; use a spoon to feather the edges gently to obtain a softer effect. Top each serving with a dollop of yoghurt sprinkled lightly with cinnamon and garnished with a sprig of mint.

APPETIZERS, DIPS AND SALADS

MEZE WI SALAT

SPICED NUT MIX
DUKKAH

MAKES 350 G/12 OZ

This is a traditional Egyptian dish which has made its way around the cusp of the Eastern Mediterranean. There is no hard and fast combination of spices or proportion of nuts – chickpeas are the resort of the poorer households.

- *150 g/5 oz shelled hazelnuts or soaked and dried chickpeas*
- *75 g/3 oz seasame seeds*
- *75 g/3 oz coriander seeds*
- *50 g/2 oz cumin seeds*
- *Salt and freshly ground pepper*
- *1.5 ml/¼ tsp dried thyme*
- *1.5 ml/¼ tsp dried marjoram*
- *Dried lemon peel*

Heat the oven to 180°C/350°F/Gas Mark 4.

Roast the hazelnuts or chickpeas on a baking tray until golden, about 8 minutes, watching carefully so that they do not burn. Remove and scrape into the bowl of a food processor fitted with a metal blade.

Spread the sesame, coriander and cumin seeds in separate parts of the baking tray, and roast until they are all coloured and toasted, about 5 minutes. Remove and scrape them into the food processor bowl. Add salt and pepper to taste, the thyme, marjoram and lemon peel, if desired. Leave the nuts and seeds to cool to just warm before grinding; otherwise the nut oils will make the mixture too wet. Pulse briefly on and off until the *dukkah* is roughly ground; do not over-process. Serve with pieces of Arab bread (*khoubz*).

The *dukkah* will keep well for about 1 week if stored in an airtight container.

AVOCADO BI TAHINI

MAKES 450 ML/1¾ CUPS

This is a standard *mezze* when ripe avocados flood the markets in Lebanon, though it is less frequently encountered in Lebanese restaurants abroad. It is particularly simple to make.

- *2 garlic cloves, crushed*
- *Salt*
- *2 ripe avocados*
- *Juice of 2 lemons*
- *75 ml/5 tbsp* tahini *paste*
- *5 ml/1 tsp ground cumin*
- *Crushed red chillies*

In a bowl, mash the garlic with salt to taste. Cut the avocados in half, take out the stone, and scoop the flesh into the bowl. Mash together with salt and garlic and a little of the lemon juice, until there are no lumps. Whip in the remaining lemon juice, the *tahini* and the ground cumin. Beat to a smooth purée.

Turn the purée into a bowl, swirl the top decoratively, and rub a few crushed chilli peppers between the fingers to sprinkle over the top. Serve with Arab bread (*khoubz*) or pitta.

SPICED ALMONDS

LOHZ

MAKES 275 G/10 OZ

Nuts play a large part in the Levantine diet, and appear as appetizers, in main courses and in desserts. Both spicy and sweet nuts appear as *mezze* or snacks; these almonds are a spicy version.

- *45 ml/3 tbsp sunflower oil*
- *275 g/10 oz whole blanched almond*
- *150 g/6 oz light brown sugar*
- *7.5 ml/1½ tsp ground cumin*
- *5 ml/1 tsp crushed chilli flakes*
- *Salt to taste*

Heat the oil over a medium-high flame until it is hot. Add the almonds, stirring together with 100 g/4 oz sugar. Toss the nuts in the sugar to coat thoroughly, and sauté until the nuts are caramelized.

Remove the nuts to a bowl and toss with the cumin, chilli flakes and salt to taste. Spread the nuts out on a baking tray to dry and, while still warm, sprinkle them with a spoonful or so of the remaining sugar to taste. Serve warm or at room temperature.

The nuts will keep for a couple of weeks if they are stored in an airtight container.

SWEET SPICED PISTACHIOS
FOSTU

MAKES 275 G/10 OZ

This is another version of nutty nibbles, this time with the accent on sweetness.

- *275 g/10 oz shelled, salted pistachios*
- *100 g/4 oz caster sugar*
- *5 ml/1 tsp ground mace*
- *5 ml/1 tsp ground cinnamon*

Place the nuts in a frying pan without any oil, and heat until they are golden, stirring frequently; this will take about 4–5 minutes. Sprinkle over the sugar, then the spices, and continue to stir until the nuts have been caramelized.

Take the nuts off the heat and spoon onto foil or a baking tray to dry. They will clump together; if desired, break apart when dry.

The nuts will keep for a couple of weeks in an airtight container.

GREEN BEANS IN OLIVE OIL
LOUBIA BI ZEIT

SERVES 6

This is a favourite, homely Lebanese dish, encountered hot, warm or cold – though most usually the last. It is an old, reliable stand-by – rather like baked beans in our cuisine.

- *450 g/1 lb green or French beans, trimmed and with strings removed, if necessary*
- *75 ml/5 tbsp olive oil*
- *1 medium onion, finely chopped*
- *3 garlic cloves, crushed*
- *200 g/7 oz tin plum tomatoes, drained and chopped*
- *1 crushed dried chilli pepper*
- *Salt and freshly ground pepper*
- *Cayenne pepper*

Bring a saucepan of water to the boil. Cut the beans into short lengths, about 5 cm/2 in, and then add them to the water, cover and simmer for 5 minutes. Drain them thoroughly.

Heat the oil in a frying pan and sauté the onion for about 5–6 minutes, until softened but not coloured. Add the garlic and stir for another 2 minutes. Stir in the tomatoes, crushed pepper and the beans. Season with salt, pepper and cayenne to taste. Pour into a serving bowl and cool. Serve the dish either at room temperature or chilled.

LEBANESE BREAD SALAD
FATTOUSH

SERVES 6

This is served as an alternative to *tabbouleh* – indeed, it makes a refreshing change when you feel you are suffering from burghul overkill!

- *2 large* khoubz *(Arab bread) or pitta, toasted*
- *Juice of 1½ lemons*
- *1 cucumber, seeded and cubed*
- *6 spring onions, chopped*
- *1 small green pepper, cored, seeded and finely chopped*
- *4 plum tomatoes, seeded, drained and chopped*
- *2 garlic cloves, crushed*
- *15 ml/1 tbsp finely chopped flat-leaved parsley*
- *15 ml/1 tbsp finely chopped coriander*
- *120 ml/4 fl oz olive oil*
- *Salt and freshly ground pepper*

Cut the toasted bread into small pieces, and place in a bowl. Squeeze over the juice from ½ lemon and toss. Set aside for 5 minutes.

In a larger bowl combine all the other ingredients, with salt and pepper to taste. Toss gently, add the bread and additional lemon juice, and combine. Serve the salad immediately.

HOT MIXED CRUSHED NUTS

MUHUMARA

MAKES 250 G/9 OZ

This is a thoroughly Lebanese version of mixed nuts, with a surprisingly spicy flavour. It is an acquired taste, but once acquired, often addictive.

- *100 g/4 oz shelled walnuts, skinned*
- *100 g/4 oz shelled pine nuts*
- *15 ml/1 tbsp sunflower oil*
- *1 garlic clove, finely chopped*
- *10 radishes, topped, tailed and finely chopped*
- *2 small fresh green chillies, seeded and finely chopped*
- *4 spring onions, finely chopped*
- *7.5 ml/½ tbsp sesame oil*
- *Cayenne pepper*
- *Salt*

With a mortar and pestle, crush the walnuts in batches until they are in very small pieces. Follow with the pine nuts. Reserve. (Alternatively, chop the nuts with a sharp knife, using a rocking motion. Then use a rolling pin to crush the nuts more finely.)

In a frying pan, warm the sunflower oil to a medium heat. Add the garlic, chopped radishes and chillies. Sauté for several minutes, making sure the garlic does not burn. Add the nuts, and toss in the oil for a minute or two, then stir in the spring onions and the sesame oil. Stir for 1 minute, season to taste with cayenne pepper and salt; turn into a bowl to cool.

Serve with Arab bread (*khoubz*) or pitta.

OLIVES BEIRUT-STYLE

Far more varieties and colours of olives are found in the Middle East than make their way to us. Round and torpedo-shaped; green, purple and black; pickled in myriad combinations of brine, vinegars and oils, they are a *mezze* staple. These are lemon-zingy.

- *60 ml/4 tbsp rich virgin olive oil*
- *10 ml/2 tsp freshly squeezed lemon juice*
- *2 cloves of garlic*
- *5 ml/1 tsp grated lemon peel*
- *2.5 ml/½ tsp dill seed*
- *400-g/14 oz tin pitted black or green olives, drained*

In a bowl or jar with a cover, combine the olive oil, lemon juice, garlic, lemon peel and dill seed. Stir thoroughly to combine. Add the olives and agitate to mix well. Cover and chill for 3 days or up to 1 week.

CHEESE BALLS
SHANKLISH

MAKES ABOUT 25–30 BALLS

In Lebanon, these cheese balls would be made of a salted Fetta-like goat cheese called *gibna arish*. Here, an unripened *chèvre* log leavened with Fetta makes a very acceptable alternative.

- *225 g/8 oz log unripened* chèvre *cheese*
- *175 g/6 oz Fetta cheese*
- *2.5 ml/½ tsp ground cumin*
- *1.5 ml/¼ tsp cayenne pepper*
- *45 ml/3 tbsp finely chopped mint or thyme leaves*
- *60 ml/4 tbsp olive oil*

Combine the cheeses, cumin and cayenne in a bowl and mash together thoroughly. Take out small spoonfuls of cheese and form into bite-sized balls. Roll the balls in the chopped herbs and chill until firm. Before serving, mound the balls on a plate and drizzle the olive oil over them.

APRICOT AND CHEESE MOUNDS

MAKES ABOUT 25 MOUNDS

The influence of the Ashkenazi Jews is evident in the use of poppy seeds in this recipe. For a more Arabic flavour, substitute toasted sesame seeds or pine nuts for the poppy seeds.

- *225 g/8 oz full-fat cream cheese*
- *50 g/2 oz shelled and skinned hazelnuts*
- *5 ml/1 tsp freshly ground pepper*
- *2.5 ml/½ tsp cayenne pepper*
- *25 ready-to-eat dried apricots*
- *60 ml/4 tbsp poppy seeds*

Preheat the oven to 180°C/350°F/Gas Mark 4.

Unwrap the cream cheese into a bowl and work until creamy. Spread the hazelnuts on a baking tray, and roast for about 8 minutes, or until toasted. Remove, chop roughly and stir into the cheese. Season with the pepper and cayenne and combine thoroughly.

Lay out the dried apricots and divide the mixture between them. Form each into a smooth mound. Roll the tops of the mounds in the poppy seeds to coat, then chill for 2–3 hours, until firm.

STUFFED BEKKAH RADISHES

MAKES ABOUT 35 RADISHES

Plump French-style radishes grown in the valleys are a popular hors-d'œuvre in Beirut. But the method of presentation is unashamedly Middle-Eastern.

- *450 g/1 lb radishes*
- *100 g/4 oz cream cheese or* Labneh *(page 53)*
- *15 ml/1 tbsp capers, chopped*
- *75 g/3 oz bottled Kalamata olive purée, drained*
- *22 ml/1½ tbsp finely chopped flat-leaved parsley*
- *Flat-leaved parsley sprigs*

Top and tail the radishes, so that they will stand on either end. Cut the radishes in half and drop them into a bowl of ice water to crisp. One at a time, using a sharp knife or a melon-baller, hollow out a small hole in each half. Return to the ice water until all the radishes are done. Remove and drain upside down on kitchen paper.

In a bowl, beat together the cheese, capers, olive purée and chopped parsley until thoroughly combined. Either pipe the filling into the halves or carefully fill with a small spoon and shape the filling with a fork. Garnish each radish with a parsley sprig.

HOUMUS

MAKES ABOUT 475 ML/16 FL OZ

This is a light, fresh version of houmus, without the strong flavour of sesame. It is more lemony and spicy; the Lebanese often serve it with a sprinkling of minced fried lamb.

- *425 g/15 oz tin chickpeas in brine, rinsed and drained*
- *2 garlic cloves, crushed*
- *30 ml/2 tbsp olive oil*
- *15 ml/1 tbsp sunflower oil*
- *45 ml/3 tbsp freshly squeezed lemon juice*
- *Salt and freshly ground pepper*
- *2.5 ml/½ tsp cayenne pepper*
- *1.5 ml/¼ tsp ground chilli*
- *30 ml/2 tbsp chopped parsley*
- *100 g/4 oz minced lamb or beef, fried with a little salt, pepper and cinnamon (optional)*

In the bowl of a food processor fitted with a metal blade, combine the chickpeas, garlic and olive oil. Process until almost smooth, stopping to push down the paste from the sides of the bowl; then add the remaining oil, lemon juice, seasoning to taste, spices and parsley. Process until very smooth, adding a little water if you wish a thinner consistency. Scrape into a bowl and swirl decoratively. Serve with Arab bread (*khoubz*) or pitta.

If desired, before serving, make a small well in the centre of the *houmus* and mound in the cinnamon-fried meat. This should be scooped up with the bread, together with the *houmus*.

HOUMUS BI TAHINI

MAKES ABOUT 475 ML/16 FL OZ

This is the more usual version of *houmus* found from Greece and Turkey to Egypt. The sesame lends a smokier flavour lacking in the previous version.

- *425 g/15 oz tin chickpeas, rinsed and drained*
- *1 garlic clove, crushed*
- *45 ml/3 tbsp* tahini *paste*
- *5 ml/1 tsp cumin*
- *30 ml/2 tbsp olive oil*
- *45 ml/3 tbsp freshly squeezed lemon juice*
- *Salt and freshly ground pepper*
- *Paprika*

In the bowl of a food processor with a metal blade, combine the chickpeas, garlic, *tahini* paste, cumin and 15 ml/1 tbsp olive oil. Process until finely chopped, push the paste down the side of the bowl, add the lemon juice, and salt and pepper to taste and process until the mixture is smooth.

Turn the purée into a bowl, smooth and swirl the surface, and drizzle with the remaining 15 ml/1 tbsp olive oil. Sprinkle with paprika, and serve with Arab bread (*khoubz*) or pitta.

COLD AUBERGINE PURÉE

MOUTABEL

MAKES ABOUT 600 ML/1 PINT

Also called *Baba Ghannoj* by the Arabs, this dip combines two smoky flavours: that of the grilled aubergine and that of the *tahini* or sesame paste. It is one of the most popular Lebanese *mezze* with foreigners, having made its way into the delicatessen department of many supermarkets.

- *2 medium aubergines, cut in half*
- *Juice of 1 lemon*
- *2 garlic cloves, crushed*
- *45 ml/3 tbsp* tahini
- *2.5 ml/½ tsp ground cumin*
- *Salt and freshly ground pepper*
- *15 ml/1 tbsp chopped flat-leaved parsley*
- *Black olives*

Prick the skins of the halved aubergines and place them flesh down on a greased baking sheet. Place them under a hot grill and grill for about 15–20 minutes, rearranging, if necessary, until the skins are blackened and blistered and the flesh is soft. Remove them from the oven, plunge them into cold water, then skin thoroughly, cutting off the skin if it sticks.

Roughly chop the aubergine flesh, and put it into the bowl of a food processor fitted with a metal blade. Add the freshly squeezed lemon juice and process for a few seconds, until combined. Scrape the mixture down the sides of the bowl and add the *tahini*, cumin, and salt and pepper to taste. Process the mixture until it becomes a smooth purée.

Turn the purée into a bowl, cover and chill slightly. Before serving, swirl the top attractively and sprinkle with the chopped parsley and a few black olives. Serve with Arab bread (*khoubz*) or pitta.

Stuffed Vine Leaves.

STUFFED VINE LEAVES
WARAH INAB

MAKES ABOUT 25 OR MORE STUFFED VINE LEAVES

Stuffed vine leaves are popular all over the eastern Mediterranean crescent, from Greece to Egypt. Unlike some of these nationalities, however, the Lebanese prefer their stuffing without meat and served cold.

- *175 g/6 oz packet vine leaves (about 35)*
- *60 ml/4 tbsp olive oil*
- *1 large onion, finely chopped*
- *30 ml/2 tbsp pine nuts*
- *50 g/2 oz long-grain rice*
- *Salt and pepper*
- *15 ml/1 tbsp raisins or currants*
- *22 ml/1½ tbsp finely chopped mint*
- *2.5 ml/½ tbsp cinnamon*
- *Juice of 2 lemons*

Remove the vine leaves from the packet, separate them, place in a large container and pour boiling water over them. Allow to soak for 15 minutes, then drain. Return to the bowl, pour cold water on them, soak for a further 10 minutes, then drain thoroughly on absorbent paper.

Heat 15 ml/1 tbsp of the olive oil in a large frying pan. Add the pine nuts and sauté, stirring, for about 4 minutes, or until the nuts are golden. Remove the pine nuts with a slotted spoon and reserve. Add another 15 ml/1 tbsp of oil to the pan, and stir in the onions. Sauté until limp and lightly coloured, about 5–6 minutes, then add the rice and salt to taste. Stir the rice until it is coated with the oil, then pour in 120 ml/4 fl oz boiling water to cover. Reduce the heat, cover, and cook over medium heat for about 5 minutes. Take off the heat and allow to sit until the water has been absorbed, and the rice is tender – about 20 minutes. Stir in the raisins or currants, pine nuts, chopped mint and cinnamon.

Lay a vine leaf flat, and spoon 30 ml/2 tbsp of the rice mixture near the stem end. Roll the leaf one turn over the mixture, then tuck in the sides of the leaf toward the centre. Contnue to roll the leaf like a cigar, until you reach the end. Squeeze the bundle to remove excess moisture. Repeat the process with the remaining leaves and stuffing.

If there are any vine leaves left over, lay them on the bottom of a lightly oiled casserole. Arrange the stuffed leaves in a single layer on top. Pour over the lemon juice and just enough hot water to cover. Drizzle over the remaining 30 ml/2 tbsp olive oil. Weigh the stuffed leaves down with a plate. Cover tightly and cook over high heat for about 4 minutes, then lower the heat and simmer for about 40 minutes. Remove from the heat, uncover and allow to cool in the cooking liquid. When cold, remove the stuffed leaves with a slotted spoon and arrange on a platter.

Serve at room temperature or chilled, together with lemon wedges to squeeze over.

TOMATO AND OLIVE SALAD
SALAT TOMATIN WI ZATUN

SERVES 4–6

This simple salad is a common accompaniment to grills and kebabs. Usually served with a classic vinaigrette or squeeze of lemon juice, it is especially good with Cumin-Lemon Dressing.

- *5–6 large beefsteak tomatoes, cored and cut into thin slices*
- *1 large red onion, finely chopped*
- *175 g/6 oz pitted black olives*
- *60 ml/4 tbsp finely chopped flat-leaved parsley*
- *Salt and pepper*
- *120 ml/4 fl oz Cumin-Lemon Dressing (page 108)*

Lay the sliced tomatoes on a serving platter, and scatter over the chopped onion and then the olives and parsley. Season with salt and pepper to taste. Pour over the dressing or lemon juice and serve the salad immediately.

RAW LAMB MIXED WITH SPICES

KIBBEH NAYEH

SERVES 6–8

This Lebanese version of steak tartare, made with lamb instead of beef and extended by the addition of burghul, is an adventure in taste worth experiencing. However, the lamb must be of exceedingly good quality and very tender. This version is traditionally served on a glass platter surrounded with cos lettuce leaves for scooping up the *kibbeh,* like edible spoons. When the mixture is rolled into balls it is called *kibbeh orayeh.*

- *450 g/1 lb tender lean lamb (tenderloin or leg), finely chopped*
- *Salt and freshly ground pepper*
- *1 large onion, chopped*
- *175 g/6 oz fine-ground burghul*
- *2.5 ml/½ tsp ground allspice*
- *5 ml/1 tsp ground cumin*
- *Cayenne pepper*
- *Olive oil*
- *5 spring onions, finely chopped*
- *Cos lettuce or chicory leaves (optional)*

Put the pieces of lamb into the bowl of a food processor fitted with a metal blade. Process until roughly ground, then add salt and pepper to taste, along with the chopped onion. Process the mixture, stopping to scrape down the sides of the bowl, until it is a smooth paste. Turn into a large bowl.

Place the burghul in another bowl, and cover with cold water. Allow to soak for about 5 minutes. Turn the cracked wheat into a sieve lined with muslin or a fine dishcloth and allow to drain for a few minutes. Pull together the ends of the muslin and squeeze out the remaining moisture. Turn the burghul into the bowl with the meat.

Sprinkle over the allspice and cumin, and add cayenne to taste. Using moistened hands, work the burghul and lamb together, kneading and pressing, until you have a grainy paste. This will take about 5 minutes. Leave for about half an hour.

If you are serving the meat as *kibbeh orayeh,* form it into small, walnut-sized balls or flatten into little patties. If you are serving *kibbeh nayeh,* together with the cos leaves, then add 15–30 ml/1–2 tbsp water, and knead the paste further in order to give it a more mousse-like consistency.

Pile the *kibbeh* onto a platter. Before serving the balls, drizzle over the olive oil. With the *kibbeh nayeh,* serve the oil separately, for guests to add as they wish. Decorate both platters with a sprinkling of chopped spring onion and lemon wedges.

MINT AND SWEET LEAF SALAD

SERVES 4–6

A contrast to the salad on page 44, this is a combination of delicate young greens and a tart oil-and-lemon dressing.

- *120 ml/4 fl oz lemon juice*
- *120 ml/4 fl oz olive oil*
- *Salt and freshly ground pepper*
- *1 small head butter lettuce, washed, dried and divided into leaves*
- *1 small head oak-leaved lettuce, washed, dried and divided into leaves*
- *50 g/2 oz whole mint leaves, washed and dried*

In a serving bowl, whisk together the lemon juice, oil and seasoning until combined. Add the lettuce leaves and mint leaves, and toss gently to coat. Serve the salad immediately.

LITTLE SPINACH PACKETS

FATAYEER

MAKES ABOUT 25 PASTRIES

Made with the same dough as the *Lahem* (page 44), these can be filled with a cheese mixture (see *Baklava* filling, page 50), meat or this sour spinach mixture, probably the most typical. Such Levantine stuffed pastries were the prototypes of the Cornish pasties and meat pies which developed in Britain after the Crusades.

- *1 portion* lahme *dough, chilled for 30 minutes (page 44)*

FILLING

- *900 g/2 lb fresh leaf spinach, washed, de-stemmed, drained and chopped*
- *45 ml/3 tbsp olive oil*
- *1 onion, grated*
- *Seeds of 1 pomegranate*
- *100 g/4 oz walnuts, crushed*
- *15 ml/1 tbsp sumac (optional)*
- *Juice of 1½ lemons*
- *Salt and freshly ground pepper*

Squeeze as much moisture as possible from the spinach. In frying pan, heat the oil and stir in the grated onion. Cook for 2 minutes, then add the spinach and stir until the spinach is thoroughly wilted. Add the seeds of the pomegranate, the walnuts, sumac if wished, and the lemon juice. Combine well, then take off the heat and set aside.

Break off the dough into 25 pieces and form into balls. On a floured board, roll the balls into small circles as thin as possible. Divide the filling among the circles. Place the filling in the centre of each circle, and bring up the sides to form three-sided packets. Pinch the top edges together.

Preheat the oven to 190°C/375°C/Gas Mark 5.

Place the pastries on oiled baking trays, and bake for 5 minutes. Then lower the heat to 180°C/350°F/ Gas Mark 4 and continue baking for a further 15–20 minutes. Remove from the oven and let them cool slightly before serving warm.

COOKED STUFFED MINCED LAMB BALLS

KIBBEH BI SHAMIYEH

MAKES ABOUT 20 STUFFED *KIBBEH*

These plump little shapes, made from cracked wheat and lamb, and stuffed with yet more lamb, are the signature dish of the Lebanese table and are still considered the test of the accomplished housewife. In a country where the food processor remains a rarity, the paste-like outer shell requires dedicated pounding in mortar and pestle, and careful treatment in stuffing and cooking to withstand breakage. We in the West have an easier time of it.

- *450 g/1 lb lean tender lamb (leg or tenderloin), finely chopped*
- *225–275 g/8–10 oz fine-ground burghul*
- *Salt and freshly ground pepper*
- *1 large onion, chopped*
- *Cayenne pepper*
- *5 ml/1 tsp cumin*

FILLING

- *30 ml/2 tbsp olive oil*
- *30 ml/2 tbsp pine nuts*
- *2 small onions, finely chopped*
- *225 g/8 oz minced lamb*
- *15 ml/1 tbsp Lebanese spice (page 16)*
- *Salt and freshly ground pepper*

- *Oil for deep-frying*

Put the small pieces of lamb in the bowl of a food processor fitted with a metal blade. Process until roughly ground, then add the chopped onion. Continue to process, stopping once or twice to scrape the mixture down the sides of the bowl, until the meat has become a smooth paste. Turn from the food processor into a large bowl.

Place 275 g/10 oz burghul in another bowl and cover with cold water. Allow to soak for about 10 minutes. Turn the cracked wheat into a sieve lined with muslin or a fine dishcloth, and allow to drain for a few minutes. Pull together the ends of the muslin and thoroughly squeeze out the remaining moisture. Turn most of the burghul into the bowl containing the meat, reserving less than a quarter.

Sprinkle cayenne pepper to taste and the cumin over the meat and burghul. Using moistened hands, work the grain and lamb together, kneading and pressing, until it is a fine paste that will take a firm shape. Work in some of the reserved burghul, if necessary. Chill for 30 minutes–1 hour.

Meanwhile make the filling. Heat the oil in a frying pan and sauté the pine nuts for about 2 minutes, until browned slightly. Remove the nuts with a slotted spoon and reserve.

Stir in the chopped onion and sauté for about 5–6 minutes until limp and just colouring. Add the minced lamb and the spice and fry until the meat is browned. Remove from the heat, drain off the excess fat, season to taste and stir in the pine nuts. Set aside.

Divide the *kibbeh* "dough" into about 20 pieces. Roll the pieces between your palms to form egg shapes. Take one "egg" and, using your index finger, make a hole from one end toward the centre, pressing and shaping the "dough" to make a largish hole with the shell as thin as possible. Fill the hole with some of the lamb filling, then pinch the open end shut, sealing in the filling. Tease the *kibbeh* into an oval with pointed ends. Repeat the stuffing process with the remaining "egg" shells and filling.

Heat the oil for frying in a large heavy saucepan or deep-fryer. Deep-fry in batches, until the *kibbeh* become a deep golden brown. Drain on absorbent paper.

Serve on a large platter with lemon wedges. The *kibbeh* can be refrigerated or frozen, and reheated in the oven when needed.

LEBANESE LAMB PIZZA

LAHEM BIL AJINE

MAKES ABOUT 25 BITE-SIZED PIZZAS

This typically Lebanese open-faced pie uses a yeast bread dough, which produces a rather floppy version of pizza. The same dough is also used to make the *fatayeer* in the recipe on page 41. Although lamb is the traditional meat to use, the pizzas can also be made with minced beef.

- *300 ml/½ pint lukewarm water*
- *20 g/4 oz fresh yeast or 15 g/½ oz dried yeast*
- *450 g/1 lb plain flour*
- *5 ml/1 tsp salt*
- *22–30 ml/1½–2 tbsp olive oil*
- *Olive oil (for coating)*

TOPPING

- *30 ml/2 tbsp olive oil*
- *450 g/1 lb Spanish or mild onions, finely chopped*
- *450 g/1 lb minced lamb*
- *400 g/14 oz tin chopped chilli tomatoes, well drained*
- *75 ml/3 fl oz tomato paste*
- *5 ml/1 tsp Lebanese spice*
- *5 ml/1 tsp brown sugar*
- *Salt and freshly ground pepper*
- *15 ml/1 tbsp finely chopped coriander*
- *15 ml/1 tbsp finely chopped parsley*

In a bowl, stir together half the water and yeast. Leave to rest for 15 minutes, or until mixture begins to foam.

In another bowl, sieve together the flour and the salt. Make a well in the middle and pour in the oil, then the yeast mixture. Using your hands, pull the flour into the liquid and begin to work into a dough. Add the remaining lukewarm water little by little to incorporate fully. When all the water has been added and the dough sticks together, remove from the bowl. On a lightly floured surface knead the dough well, for about 15 minutes, until it becomes shiny and elastic, about 15 minutes. Pat the dough into a ball.

Pour a little oil in the bowl, place the dough in it and turn the ball to coat it. Remove the ball to a warm place and cover with a damp cloth. Leave for about 2½ hours, until it has doubled in size.

To make the filling, heat the oil in a frying pan and add the onions. Sauté until limp and lightly coloured. In a bowl, combine the meat, well-drained tomatoes, tomato paste, spice, sugar, salt and pepper to taste, and the herbs. Add the cooked onions and mix the ingredients using the hands.

With dampened hands, break off pieces of the dough and form into 25 balls. Press each ball between the hands, flattening into a small disc, and place on an oiled baking tray. Divide the topping between the pizza bases, spreading evenly. Bake in a preheated 220°C/425°F/Gas Mark 7 oven, for about 10 minutes, until a little puffy and lightly coloured. Remove from the oven and serve immediately.

The *lahem* can be refrigerated or frozen and reheated in the oven when needed.

MIXED BITTER LEAF SALAD

SERVES 4–6

Taking their cue from the biblical reference to bitter herbs, this salad has a palate-awakening effect. The addition of Pistachio Dressing, however, makes the result far more lip-smacking.

- *2 medium heads chicory, rinsed, dried and broken into leaves*
- *15 inner leaves of cos lettuce, rinsed, dried, broken into leaves and roughly chopped*
- *1 bunch watercress, washed, dried and with excess stems removed*
- *175 ml/6 fl oz Pistachio Dressing (page 109)*

Arrange the chicory leaves around the edges of a shallow serving bowl. In the centre, mix together the cos lettuce and watercress. Pour over the Pistachio Dressing, toss gently and serve immediately.

SPICED FRUIT MEATBALLS

MAKES 25–30 BALLS

Mouth-watering meatballs such as these occur in many variations throughout the Middle East. The inclusion of fruit is a preference of Turkey and the Levant, where the mingling of savoury and sweet is more common. Currants or dates can be substituted for the sultanas. This goes particularly well with Yoghurt Sauce (page 108).

- *25 g/1 oz fresh white breadcrumbs*
- *120 ml/4 oz yoghurt*
- *45 ml/3 tbsp olive oil*
- *50 g/2 oz pine nuts*
- *50 g/2 oz sultanas, soaked in hot water and drained*
- *465 ml/3 tbsp finely chopped spring onion*
- *1 clove garlic, finely chopped*
- *5 ml/1 tsp ground cinnamon*
- *5 ml/1 tsp ground allspice*
- *5 ml/1 tsp salt*
- *450 g/1 lb minced lamb or beef*

In a bowl, mix together the breadcrumbs and yoghurt and leave to soak for 10 minutes. In a frying pan heat 15 ml/1 tbsp of the oil, and sauté the pine nuts until lightly golden, about 4–5 minutes. Drain on absorbent paper and add to the yoghurt mix.

Stir in the sultanas, spring onion, garlic, spices and salt. Add the meat and combine thoroughly using your hands. Chill the meat mixture for 30 minutes.

Make about 30 small balls from the mixture. Heat the oil and sauté the balls in batches for about 6 minutes, turning to ensure they brown all over. Transfer to absorbent paper to drain, and keep warm while cooking the remaining balls.

The balls may be refrigerated or frozen and reheated in the oven when required.

ANCHOVY AND EGG FRITTERS

AGGAH BI ANSHUGA

SERVES 6–8

***Eggah,* as it is known in Egypt where it is particularly popular, occurs in a number of guises throughout the region. A form of omelet, it is sometimes made with flour in Lebanon, becoming a *beignet.* Here it is extended with potato and cut into wedges.**

- *30 ml/2 tbsp olive or sunflower oil*
- *5 spring onions, finely chopped*
- *6 anchovy fillets, washed, drained, dried and finely chopped*
- *1 large potato, grated*
- *5 ml/1 tsp cumin*
- *45 ml/3 tbsp finely chopped flat-leaved parsley*
- *6 eggs*
- *Salt and freshly ground pepper*

Heat 30 ml/2 tbsp oil in a large frying pan with a lid. When hot, add the chopped onions and sauté until they are limp. Take off the heat and remove the onions with a slotted spoon to a large bowl.

Add the chopped anchovy, grated potato, cumin and parsley to the bowl, and mix together. One by one, beat in the eggs. Season according to taste.

Put the pan back on the heat, turning to coat it with the oil. Pour in the egg mixture, turn the heat to low, and cover. Cook for about 15–20 minutes, until the eggs are just set.

Uncover the pan, put a plate over the top, and invert the flat omelet onto the plate. Carefully slip back into the pan and cook for a further 3 minutes.

Remove the omelet, cut into thin wedges, and roll up each wedge, fat end to thin point of the triangle. Secure with a cocktail stick. Serve warm or cold.

SPICED CHICKPEA BALLS

FALAFEL

MAKES ABOUT 25–30 BALLS

Although most closely associated with Israel, *falafel* are eaten all over the Middle East and appear on every Lebanese restaurant menu. The *falafel* can be made using only bread (and no burghul), which gives them a denser consistency.

- *75 g/3 oz Arab bread* (khoubz) *or pitta, torn into shreds*
- *75 g/3 oz fine-ground burghul*
- *400 g/14 oz tin chickpeas, rinsed and drained*
- *3 garlic cloves, crushed*
- *1 small onion, chopped*
- *5 ml/1 tsp crushed red pepper, flaked*
- *10 ml/2 tsp chopped coriander*
- *5 ml/1 tsp lemon juice*
- *5 ml/1 tsp ground cumin*
- *Salt and freshly ground pepper*
- *Oil for deep frying*

In a small bowl, combine the shredded bread with water to cover. Leave for about 15 minutes. In another bowl, combine the burghul with water to cover. Leave for 15 minutes also.

Meanwhile, in the bowl of a food processor fitted with a metal blade, combine the drained chickpeas, the garlic, onion, spices and lemon juice. Process, stopping to push the paste down the sides of the bowl, until it is smooth.

Drain the bread and the burghul. Squeeze both as dry as possible, separately, in muslin or a fine dishcloth. Add the bread to the chickpea paste and process until it is as smooth as possible.

Scrape the paste into a bowl. Add the burghul, season with salt and pepper to taste, and thoroughly combine the mixture with the hands. Shape into small nut-sized balls, arrange on greaseproof paper and chill – in layers if necessary – for about 2 hours.

Heat the oil in a deep-fryer or saucepan until just smoking at about 190°C/375°F. Deep-fry the balls for about 4 minutes each, until golden brown. Drain the balls on kitchen paper.

Serve the *felafel* warm with *Taratoor bi Tahini* (page 106) or Yoghurt and Cucumber Sauce (page 108).

COOKED CHEESE WITH BREAD

KALLAJE

MAKES 12 ROUNDS

This is an adaptation of the plain grilled cheese on toasted pitta served at Lebanese, Greek and Turkish restaurants, which is often unappetizingly rubbery and lacking in any taste other than that of salt. This version allows the distinctive flavours of the region to assert themselves.

- *45 ml/3 tbsp* semnah *or butter, melted*
- *6 fresh pitta or pocket bread*
- *675 g/1½ lb Kasseri or Hallomi cheese, grated*
- *1 garlic clove, finely chopped*
- *5 ml/1 tsp fresh marjoram, finely chopped*
- *120 ml/4 oz fresh lemon juice*

Lightly brush two muffin tins with some of the melted *semnah* or butter. From each pitta, cut two circles of bread to fit two muffin cups. Repeat with the remaining pittas. Place a bread circle in each muffin cup and brush with the remaining *semnah*.

In a bowl, mix together the cheese, garlic, marjoram and lemon juice. Take handfuls of the mixture and top the pitta rounds with it.

Place the muffin tins in an oven preheated to 200°C/400°F/Gas Mark 6, and bake for about 10 minutes, or until the cheese is bubbling and slightly browned. Serve immediately.

LAMB CRESCENT PASTRIES

LAMB SAMBOUSEK

MAKES ABOUT 25 PASTRIES

The following recipe includes a traditional meat filling. The cheese filling used in the savoury *baklava* could be used instead, omitting the tomatoes and substituting 30–45 ml/2–3 tbsp dill or mint.

- *175 g/6 oz plain flour*
- *Salt*
- *15 ml/1 tbsp sunflower oil*
- *1 onion, finely chopped*
- *1 garlic clove, finely chopped*
- *375 g/12 oz minced lamb*
- *30 ml/2 tbsp pine nuts*
- *Salt and freshly ground black pepper*
- *15 ml/1 tbsp Lebanese spice (page 16)*
- *30 ml/2 tbsp chopped mint*
- *5 ml/1 tsp sugar*
- *30 ml/2 tbsp lemon juice*
- *1 egg, beaten*
- *Oil for deep-frying*
- *120 ml/4 fl oz warm water*

Sieve the flour, salted to taste, into a bowl. Slowly add the water, mixing with a knife. Then work with the hands and remove from the bowl. Knead on a floured surface for 5 minutes, until smooth. Wrap in plastic film and chill for 30 minutes.

In a frying pan heat the oil and sauté the onion and garlic until limp and lightly coloured. Stir in the minced lamb, and cook until browned all over. Drain off the excess fat. Add the pine nuts, salt and pepper to taste, the spice and mint, and the sugar. Cook for a further 2–3 minutes, then take off the heat. Stir in the lemon juice.

To make the pastries, divide the dough into about 25 little balls. Roll out one on a floured board into a small circle, spoon a little of the filling into the centre of the circle, dampen the edges with a little beaten egg, and fold the pastry over the filling. Crimp the edges with a fork. Repeat the process with the remaining balls and filling.

Heat the oil for deep-frying. When it has reached 190°C/375°F, drop the pastries in, 3–4 at a time. Cook until golden brown and remove with a slotted spoon on to absorbent paper to drain. Bring the oil back to the correct heat, and continue until all the pastries have been fried (adding a little more oil when necessary). Keep warm until ready to serve.

The pastries may be refrigerated or frozen after frying. They can be reheated in the oven when needed.

A modern restaurant by an old bridge, Jezir El Khadi.

SAVOURY BAKLAVA

SERVES 6

This mouth-watering cheese-and-onion pie makes a delicious hors-d'œuvre at a drinks party, on its own or paired with *Kibbeg bi Sanieh.* The sun-dried tomato is a new introduction from Italian residents of Lebanon, but it marries wonderfully with the cheese. The *baklava* can be served cold, but is at its best warm – not piping hot.

- *175 g/6 oz* samneh *(page 14) or butter*
- *2 onions, finely chopped*
- *2 garlic cloves, finely chopped*
- *1.5 ml/¼ tsp dry marjoram*
- *1.5 ml/¼ tsp dry thyme*
- *225 g/8 oz Fetta cheese*
- *225 g/8 oz* Labneh *(page 53)*
- *2 eggs*
- *30 ml/2 tbsp milk*
- *50 g/2 oz sun-dried tomatoes in oil, drained and finely chopped*
- *Salt and freshly ground pepper*
- *225 g/8 oz phyllo pastry (in 8 × 12 in/20 × 30 cm sheets)*

In a frying pan, warm 30 ml/2 tbsp of the *smenah* or butter. Add the onions and sauté, for about 5 minutes, stirring throughout. Add the garlic and herbs, and continue to cook until the onions are limp and lightly coloured. Scrape into a bowl.

Add the two cheeses and the eggs to the onion mixture, beating to combine. Stir in the milk, then the sun-dried tomatoes and seasoning to taste. Continue to beat until everything is well mixed.

Melt the remaining *smenah* or butter carefully over medium heat. Unwrap the phyllo sheets and cover them with a wet cloth to prevent drying while making the *baklava*. Brush the bottom of a shallow baking dish or pan with butter. (It should be large enough just to accommodate the phyllo sheets. If slightly smaller, overlap the edges of the pastry as you "build" the pie.) Lay two sheets of phyllo in the pan and brush with the melted *smenah*. Lay two more sheets on top and brush with more *smenah*. Continue until you have used half the phyllo.

Spread the cheese filling evenly over the pastry. Cover with two sheets of phyllo, brush with *smenah*, and add two more sheets. Continue as before, until you have used all the phyllo. Brush the top generously with the *smenah*, and cut the pie into bite-sized diamond-shaped pieces.

Bake in an oven preheated to 200°C/400°F/Gas Mark 6 for about 45 minutes, or until the top is golden and the filling cooked. Allow to cool slightly, then re-cut the *baklava* and serve it.

LEBANESE COLESLAW

SALAT MALFOOF

SERVES 6–8

This cabbage salad has a strong garlic flavour, and complements grills and barbecued meats wonderfully.

- *2 garlic cloves*
- *5 ml/1 tsp salt*
- *120 ml/4 fl oz fresh lemon juice*
- *120 ml/4 fl oz olive oil*
- *1 small Dutch white cabbage (about 375 g/12 oz), cored and shredded*
- *45 ml/3 tbsp fresh mint, shredded*
- *45 ml/3 tbsp caraway seeds*

Using a mortar and pestle, mash the garlic with the salt until you have a paste. Slowly work in the lemon juice. Transfer the sauce to a large bowl and whisk in the olive oil adding only a small amount at a time, until the dressing is emulsified.

Add the shredded cabbage, mint and caraway seeds, and fold into the dressing. Serve immediately.

DEEP-FRIED ALMOND SQUID

MAKES ABOUT 25 RINGS

Squid is another favourite of all Mediterranean peoples, and the Lebanese are no exception. This *meze* is lovely and crunchy and is especially well complemented by a dip of Almond Sauce (page 95).

- *450 g/1 lb squid bodies, cleaned, rinsed and patted dry*
- *75 g/3 oz plain flour*
- *Salt and freshly ground pepper*
- *Cayenne pepper*
- *75 g/3 oz fine-ground burghul, soaked and drained in a lined colander overnight*
- *50 g/2 oz finely chopped blanched almonds*
- *2 eggs*
- *Oil for deep frying*

With a sharp knife, slice the squid sacs into rings and reserve.

Measure the flour onto a plate, and mix in salt, pepper and a little ground cayenne to taste. On another plate put the burghul, which should now be dry. Stir the chopped almonds into the burghul. Crack the eggs into a shallow bowl and beat quickly.

Take the squid rings one by one and dust them with the flour. Then dip the rings into the beaten egg and, finally, coat with the burghul-almond mixture. Place the rings in a single layer on a platter or tray and chill for 1 hour.

Heat the oil to 180°C/360°F, and deep-fry the rings in batches until golden. Keep warm until served.

STUFFED FISH BALLS

KIBBEH SAMAK

MAKES ABOUT 20 BALLS

In the coastal ports of Sidon and Tyre, tasty alternatives to lamb *kibbeh* take the form of deep-fried fish patties and balls. This is one variation with a light, fruity filling.

- *450 g/1 lb fine-ground burghul*
- *1 large onion, chopped*
- *675 g/1½ lb white fish fillets, skinned*
- *2 tbsp lemon juice*
- *Salt and freshly ground pepper*

FILLING

- *1 large onion, finely chopped*
- *15 ml/1 tbsp oil*
- *45 ml/3 tbsp finely chopped coriander*
- *50 g/2 oz chopped ready-to-eat apricots*
- *25 g/1 oz finely chopped dates*

- *Oil for deep-frying*
- *Lemon wedges*
- *Ice water*

Put the burghul in a bowl and cover with cold water. Leave for 10 minutes.

Put the chopped onion in the bowl of a food processor fitted with a metal blade. Process until the onion has been thoroughly chopped, then add the fish fillets, and continue to process until the fish is a paste. Add the lemon juice and seasoning to the processor, and blend until you have a smooth purée.

Drain the burghul in a sieve lined with muslin or a fine dishcloth. Then take up the end of the cloth and twist it to squeeze out all the excess moisture. Add the dried burghul in batches to the fish purée, processing between additions. You should end up with a workable dough. If necessary, add a little ice water to make it more malleable.

To make the filling, fry the onion in the oil until it is lightly coloured and limp. Stir in the coriander, chopped apricots and chopped dates. Take off the heat and reserve.

With moistened hands, divide the fish dough into about 20 pieces and roll them into balls. Using your index finger, make a hole in each ball and stuff with a little of the filling. Re-form the ball around the filling and pat into shape.

Heat the oil for deep-frying, and drop the fish balls into it a few at a time. Fry until the balls are golden, and remove to absorbent paper to drain. Serve warm or at room temperature with lemon wedges. They can be refrigerated or frozen and reheated, if necessary.

The *kibbeh* are also delicious dipped into *Taratoor bi Tahini* (page 106) or Yoghurt Sauce (page 108).

Stuffed fish balls

YOGHURT CREAM CHEESE DIP

LABNEH

MAKES ABOUT 1.15 L/2 PINTS

Usually made with goat's milk yoghurt in Lebanon, this mild but flavourful cream cheese dip is ubiquitous on the Lebanese table. It is a popular *meze* dip and can be turned into a more substantial variation by the addition of one or more of the following ingredients: chopped cucumber, spring onions, sweet peppers or chillies.

- *1.15 l/2 pints natural yoghurt (goat or sheep preferred)*
- *5 ml/1 tsp salt*
- *15 ml/1 tbsp olive oil*
- *Paprika*

In a bowl, combine the yoghurt and the salt, and whip to mix thoroughly. Line a colander with damp muslin or a clean, fine-weave dishcloth. Let it drain in this position for a while, then tie the corners of the cloth together and hang it from a tap over the sink for about 12 hours or overnight.

To serve, decant the drained cheese into a bowl. Swirl the top decoratively and drizzle the olive oil over the cheese. Sprinkle with the paprika. Serve with Arab bread (*khoubz*) or pitta.

RICE AND PISTACHIO SALAD

SERVES 6

This salad is a visitor – from the eastern borders and Iran – that came to stay. Rice is very much a secondary grain in Lebanon; a refinement of Beirut and the larger towns, which can boast a more cosmopolitan clientele than the masses who rely on burghul. (This salad is exceptionally delicious made with 60 ml/4 tbsp pistachio oil substituted for the olive oil used to toss the salad. It can be obtained in some delicatessens, but is unfortunately very expensive.)

- *375 g/12 oz long-grain rice*
- *75 ml/5 tbsp olive oil*
- *Salt and freshly ground pepper*
- *45 ml/3 tbsp fresh lemon juice*
- *5 ml/1 tsp grated lemon peel*
- *5 ml/1 tsp pomegranate seeds*
- *45 ml/3 tbsp finely chopped flat-leaved parsley*
- *4 spring onions, finely chopped*
- *50 g/2 oz shelled pistachios*

Sauté the rice in 15 ml/1 tbsp olive oil, stirring to coat thoroughly. (If substituting pistachio oil for the dressing, sauté the rice in sunflower oil instead of olive oil.) When the rice is transparent, add salt to taste and boiling water to cover, bring to a boil, and cover. Reduce the heat for 5 minutes and simmer, then turn off the heat and let the rice sit until it has absorbed all the water and is tender – about 25 minutes. (If necessary, add a drop or two of boiling water if the rice is still not tender. Stir, and leave for another 5 minutes.) Put the rice aside in a serving bowl to dry and cool.

In a small bowl, whisk together the lemon juice and the remaining olive oil (or pistachio oil). Season to taste, and add the lemon peel and pomegranate seeds. Set the mixture aside.

To the bowl with the rice add the parsley, spring onions and pistachios. Stir in the lemon dressing. Cover and chill for at least 2 hours before serving.

SMALL COURGETTE PUFFS

AGGAH BI KOUSA

MAKES ABOUT 25–30 *AGGAHS*

Unlike the *aggah* above, this is less of an omelet and more of a *beignet.* It is light and a perfect accompaniment to drinks as well as a delightful *meze*.

- *6 small courgettes, washed, trimmed and roughly chopped*
- *100 g/4 oz butter, cubed*
- *175 ml/6 fl oz water*
- *2 garlic cloves, finely chopped*
- *100 g/4 oz plain flour*
- *4 eggs*
- *45 ml/3 tbsp finely chopped parsley*
- *1.5 ml/¼ tsp cayenne*
- *Salt and freshly ground pepper*
- *Oil for deep-frying*

Steam the courgettes in a steamer or saucepan with a little water. Remove from the heat when softened, and mash until smooth. Reserve.

Put the butter, water and garlic into a heavy saucepan. Bring to the boil.

Pour in the flour all at once, and stir with a wooden spoon or spatula until the batter leaves the sides of the saucepan. Scrape into a bowl and beat in the eggs, one at a time, until the batter is shiny. Beat in the mashed courgettes, together with the parsley, cayenne and seasoning to taste.

Heat the oil in a heavy saucepan or deep-fryer. Drop in the courgette batter, teaspoonfuls at a time, and fry for about 5 minutes, until golden. Remove when done with a slotted spoon, and drain on absorbent paper. Keep the *beignets* warm while you finish frying the remaining batter. Serve warm with lemon wedges or Yoghurt Sauce (page 108) for dipping.

CRACKED WHEAT AND HERB SALAD

TABBOULEH

SERVES 6

Probably the best-known of all Lebanese dishes outside the country, this salad has become a staple of summer parties and picnics in Britain, France and the United States, and is found in the display cabinet of every delicatessen. A true *tabbouleh,* however, customarily has more herbs to grain than is usually found in our Westernized versions.

- *175 g/6 oz medium burghul*
- *5 ml/1 tsp salt*
- *Juice of 2 lemons*
- *300 g/11 oz finely chopped flat-leaved parsley*
- *200 g/7 oz finely chopped mint*
- *30 ml/2 tbsp finely chopped spring onion*
- *60 ml/2 fl oz olive oil*
- *3 plum tomatoes, seeded, drained and chopped*
- *1/3 cucumber, seeded and finely chopped*
- *Salt and freshly ground pepper*

In a large bowl, soak the burghul in salted boiling water (enough to cover) for 10 minutes, then rinse and drain thoroughly. Squeeze out any remaining moisture in a dishcloth or muslin. Transfer the burghul to another bowl, and add the juice of one lemon. Leave to soften for 1 hour.

To make the salad, combine the parsley, mint, spring onion, oil, tomato and cucumber in a large bowl. Gently stir in the burghul, combining well. Season to taste and add more lemon juice, as desired. Chill slightly before serving.

LENTIL SALAD

SALAT 'AADS

SERVES 4–6

This salad is made with the earthy brown lentil beloved of peasants and farm workers. Despite the fact that they are considered the "food of the poor", lentils have an honoured place in Lebanese cookery, and have made their way from the East and Middle East into European *cuisine bourgeoise.*

- *225 g/8 oz dried brown lentils, soaked for 1 hour*
- *1 crushed red chilli*
- *5 ml/1 tsp cumin seed*
- *1 bay leaf*
- *75 ml/5 tbsp olive oil*
- *Juice of 1 lemon*
- *2 garlic cloves, crushed*
- *Salt and freshly ground pepper*
- *45 ml/3 tbsp finely chopped flat-leaved parsley*

Drain the lentils and pick them over for stones and debris. Rinse again and place in a saucepan of water to cover, together with the chilli, cumin seeds and bay leaf. Bring to the boil, cover and simmer for about 30 minutes, or until tender. Drain thoroughly.

In a large bowl whisk together the oil, lemon juice, garlic and salt and pepper to taste. Add the warm lentils and the chopped parsley. Toss to combine, allow to cool, and chill for a couple of hours or overnight. (If there are leftovers, the lentils can be puréed or mashed, thinned with olive oil and more lemon juice, spiced with cayenne and fresh chopped coriander, and served as a dip.

SLICED CUCUMBER SALAD
SALAT KHIYAR

SERVES 6

Unlike the Arabic population of the Levant, the large Maronite and other Christian communities have no prohibition against alcohol. Wine, and here its derivative vinegar, feature in their recipes.

- *2 large cucumbers, peeled, halved, seeded and thinly sliced*
- *Salt and freshly ground pepper*
- *120 ml/8 tbsp finely chopped fresh mint*
- *60 ml/4 tbsp finely chopped flat-leaved parsley*
- *5 ml/1 tsp orange blossom water or grated rind of ½ orange*
- *120 ml/4 fl oz olive oil*
- *120 ml/4 fl oz red wine vinegar*
- *57 ml/5 tbsp caster sugar*

Place the cucumber slices in a colander and toss liberally with salt. Leave to drain for 30 minutes.

In a large bowl put the parsley and orange water or rind. Whisk in the olive oil, red wine vinegar and the sugar until combined, and until the sugar has dissolved. Mix in the mint.

Dry the cucumber slices with absorbent paper, then add to the vinaigrette. Toss gently to combine. Chill for several hours or overnight before serving.

CHICKPEA SALAD

SALAT HOUMUS

SERVES 6

This salad is delicious as a first course or as an accompaniment to kebabs or other lamb dishes.

- *90 ml/6 tbsp olive oil*
- *1 garlic clove, crushed*
- *1 large Spanish onion, thinly sliced*
- *1 red pepper, cored, seeded and chopped*
- *15 ml/1 tbsp dried thyme*
- *2.5 ml/½ tsp cumin seeds*
- *45 ml/3 tbsp lemon juice*
- *400 g/14 oz chickpeas, drained and rinsed*
- *Salt and freshly ground pepper*
- *2 hard-boiled eggs, chopped*
- *Flat-leaved parsley*

Heat the oil in a saucepan and sauté the garlic clove and onion over medium heat, until limp and lightly coloured. After a minute or two add the red pepper, thyme and cumin seeds. Take off the heat and scrape the contents of the pan, including the oil, into a large bowl. Whisk in the lemon juice.

Stir the rinsed and drained chickpeas into the dressing, season to taste, and gently fold in the chopped egg. Turn the beans into a serving bowl and garnish with the flat-leaved parsley.

SWEET-AND-SOUR AUBERGINE
BAZINJAN RAHIB

SERVES 6

This is the popular aubergine in another guise – one often served at the *mezze* table. It lacks the smoky flavour of *moutabal,* relying on texture and flavour contrast for appeal.

- *2 medium aubergines, trimmed and cubed*
- *Salt*
- *4 garlic cloves, crushed*
- *2 large, mild yellow onions, chopped*
- *120 ml/4 fl oz olive oil*
- *5 ml/1 tsp paprika*
- *10 ml/2 tsp ground cumin*
- *15 ml/1 tbsp light brown sugar*
- *3 medium tomatoes, seeded and chopped*
- *Juice of 1 lemon*
- *60 ml/4 tbsp finely chopped coriander*

In a colander toss the cubed aubergine with plenty of salt. Leave to drain for 30 minutes. Pat dry.

Line a large baking pan with aluminium foil. In a bowl combine the aubergine, garlic cloves, chopped onions, olive oil, cumin, paprika and sugar. Toss together gently until the aubergine is thoroughly coated with the oil and spices. Spread the aubergine in the lined baking pan, and bake in a preheated 200°C/400°F/Gas Mark 6 oven for about 40 minutes, stirring twice as they cook.

Add the tomatoes to the pan, tossing to combine, and moisten with a little more oil, if necessary. Return to the oven for a further 15–20 minutes, until the aubergine and tomatoes are both very soft.

Turn the cooked vegetables into a large bowl. Add the lemon juice and chopped coriander, stir to mix thoroughly, and bring to room temperature or chill slightly before serving.

CUCUMBER AND YOGHURT SALAD
CAÇIK

SERVES 6

Called *tzatziki* in Greece, this creamy, slightly bitter salad is popular all over the Middle East, though it retains its Turkish name.

- *1 cucumber, peeled, halved, seeded and diced*
- *Salt*
- *2 garlic cloves, crushed*
- *450 ml/¾ pint Greek-style yoghurt*
- *Freshly ground white pepper*
- *60 ml/4 tbsp finely chopped fresh mint*

Put the diced cucumber in a colander, sprinkle liberally with salt and toss to coat. Leave to drain for 30 minutes. Meanwhile, in a bowl, combine the garlic, yoghurt, pepper to taste and the mint. Chill the mixture to let the flavours mingle.

Dry the drained cucumber with absorbent paper and add to the yoghurt dressing. Toss gently to mix and serve immediately.

PARSNIP AND DATE SALAD

SERVES 4–6

This is an unusual salad, making use of a peasant stand-by – parsnip – and that manna of the desert, the date. It makes an interesting complement to meat salads (like the one following) or kebabs.

- *6 medium parsnips, topped, tailed and peeled*
- *24 plump medjul dates, pitted*
- *60 ml/4 tsp lemon juice*
- *15 ml/1 tbsp light brown sugar*
- *120 ml/4 fl oz Greek-style yoghurt*

Finely grate the parsnip into a large bowl. Chop the dates roughly and add them to the bowl. In a small bowl whisk together the lemon juice, sugar and yoghurt, until the sugar is dissolved.

Fold the dressing into the parsnips and dates. Chill slightly and serve.

BEEF AND BARLEY SALAD

SERVES 4–6

Beef is far less usual in Lebanese cooking than lamb, which thrives on the rugged foothills and dry coastal plains. But demand for beef in hotels and restaurants in towns has resulted in a successful marriage of Western tastes and local flavourings. Barley is an introduction from the Turkish and Aremenian traditions, the sumac from Syrian. This salad takes 2–3 days to make.

- *100 g/4 oz sumac seeds*
- *60 ml/4 tbsp olive oil*
- *30 ml/2 tbsp red wine vinegar*
- *675 g/1½ lb sirloin, 2.5 cm/1 in thick*
- *750 ml/1¼ pints chicken stock*
- *175 g/6 oz pearl barley, rinsed and drained*
- *1 red onion, finely chopped*
- *75 g/3 oz slivered blanched almonds, toasted*
- *225 g/8 oz seedless green grapes, halved*
- *Salt and freshly ground pepper*
- *Watercress*
- *Cucumber slices and radishes*
- *Lemon quarters*
- *2.5 ml/½ tsp coriander*

Make sumac juice by soaking the seeds in 350 ml/12 fl oz boiling water for 20–30 minutes. Strain, discard the seeds and bottle.

In a bowl, whisk together the olive oil, vinegar and 60 ml/2 tbsp sumac juice (the remainder can be refrigerated or frozen for future use). Pour the marinade into a large plastic bag, add the sirloin, seal the bag, and shake to coat the beef. Put the bag into a bowl and chill the meat in the marinade overnight.

To cook the meat, grill on a barbecue or under a hot grill for about 8–10 minutes on each side, basting with the marinade, until the meat is seared and just cooked on the outside but pink inside. Let the meat cool and chill, covered, several hours or overnight.

Meanwhile, make the barley. Bring the chicken stock to the boil, add the barley, cover and simmer until tender – about 30 minutes. Drain, cool and chill overnight.

To assemble the salad, slice the meat into thin strips. Reserve a few strips and put the remainder in the bowl. Add the barley, red onion, almonds, halved grapes and coriander. Moisten the salad with a little of the marinade, season with salt and pepper to taste, and arrange on a bed of watercress. Arrange the reserved beef strips on top and garnish with cucumber slices, radishes and lemon quarters.

Parsnip and date salad

MELON SALAD WITH CARDAMOM

SERVES 6

This can be made with orange or green/white melons, but is most flavourful made with juicy bright Charantais or cantaloupe melons. This can be served as a fruity accompaniment to the main course – particularly lamb dishes – or as a light dessert.

- *150 ml/¼ pint Greek-style yoghurt*
- *2.5 ml/½ tsp ground cardamom*
- *7.5 ml/1½ tsp honey*
- *75 ml/3 fl oz lemon or lime juice*
- *2 medium melons, peeled, seeded and cubed (or shaped into balls with a melon baller)*

In a small bowl, whisk together the yoghurt, cardamom, honey and juice until thoroughly mixed. Place the melon balls or cubes in a serving bowl, pour over the dressing and gently toss the salad to combine. Serve immediately.

GRAPEFRUIT AND AVOCADO COMPOTE

SERVES 6

Served with Satsuma Dressing or a lemony vinaigrette, this makes a delicious first course or accompaniment to a meat salad. An Israeli-style dish, it found favour in the hotel cuisine that once flourished in Beirut.

- *2 sweet pink grapefruit, peeled and with pith removed, divided into segments*
- *2 large ripe avocados, peeled and stoned, cut into cubes*
- *120 ml/4 fl oz Satsuma Dressing (page 112) or Classic Vinaigrette (page 107)*
- *30 ml/2 tbsp blanched almond slices, toasted*

In a serving bowl, combine the pink grapefruit and the avocado. Pour over the dressing and toss gently to combine. Scatter over the toasted almonds and serve immediately.

SWEET-AND-SOUR COURGETTES

KOUSA BE ZEIT

SERVES 6

A relative of the aubergine, the courgette has not quite attained the popularity of that vegetable in Lebanon. However, this cooked salad is one dish that finds appreciative appetites, either as a *mezze* or side dish. This Francophile version also uses wine vinegar as well as lemon juice, but the juice alone may be used to impart a more Arabian flavour.

- *120 ml/4 fl oz olive oil*
- *1 red onion, finely chopped*
- *900 g/2 lb courgettes, scrubbed trimmed and cut into thin 5 cm/2 in strips*
- *30 ml/2 tbsp white wine vinegar*
- *30 ml/2 tbsp lemon juice*
- *30 ml/2 tbsp caster sugar*
- *5 ml/1 tsp coriander seeds*
- *5 ml/1 tsp dill seeds*
- *2.5 ml/½ tsp cinnamon*
- *Salt and pepper*
- *30 ml/2 tbsp pine nuts, toasted*
- *30 ml/2 tbsp currants*

Heat the oil in a frying pan and sauté the onion gently for about 5 minutes, until softened but not coloured. Stir in the courgettes and cook for a further 10 minutes, until also softened. Pour in the vinegar and lemon juice, and stir in the sugar, coriander and dill seeds, cinnamon and salt and pepper to taste. Simmer for about 5 minutes, then add the pine nuts and currants. Cook for a further 4–5 minutes, until the liquid has evaporated somewhat and the courgettes have become glazed.

Chill for several hours or overnight before serving.

BEETROOT SALAD

SALAT BANGAR

SERVES 4–6

This combination of a dairy product and beetroot has echoes of Russian and Polish cuisine, although those countries would use sour cream rather than yoghurt. The addition of olive oil and cumin, however, is distinctly Levantine, while the optional ricotta – a type of which is made in the Lebanon – provides a richer texture.

- *30 ml/2 tbsp olive oil*
- *30 ml/2 tbsp lemon juice*
- *250 ml/8 fl oz Greek-style yoghurt*
- *2.5 ml/½ tsp cumin seeds*
- *50 g/2 oz ricotta cheese (optional)*
- *Salt and freshly ground pepper*
- *450 g/1 lb cooked beetroot, thinly sliced*
- *Chopped mint leaves*

In a large bowl, whisk together the oil and lemon juice with a fork. Stir in the yoghurt and cumin seeds. With the back of the fork, mash in the ricotta, if used. Season the mixture to taste. Gently fold in the beetroot.

Transfer the salad to a serving bowl and garnish with chopped mint leaves. Chill or serve immediately.

FISH

SAMAK

CLAMS OR MUSSELS TYRE-STYLE

SERVES 4–6

Tyre was renowned in ancient times for its purple dye, reserved for Roman aristocrats and derived from the crushed shells of whelks. But that was not the only shellfish that thrived on the sea-shelf fronting the harbour. Mussels, several types of clam, shrimp and crayfish graced the Tyrean table and were transported inland. The tradition remains.

- *1 garlic clove, crushed*
- *1 small red onion, thinly sliced*
- *250 ml/8 fl oz white wine*
- *900 g/2 lb prairie clams or small mussels*
- *4 plum tomatoes, peeled, seeded and chopped*
- *30 ml/2 tbsp lemon juice*
- *15 ml/1 tbsp* semnah *or butter*
- *30 ml/1 tbsp finely chopped fresh coriander*

Put the garlic and chopped onion into the wine in a deep saucepan. Bring to the boil, simmer for 2 minutes, then add the mussels or clams. Bring back to the boil, lower the heat and simmer, covered, for about 5 minutes, or until the shellfish open. Discard any mussels or clams that have not opened.

Remove the shellfish to a serving bowl and keep them warm. Add the tomatoes to the cooking liquid, and mash them into it. Bring it back to the boil and reduce slightly. Just before serving, stir in the lemon juice, *semnah* or butter, and the chopped coriander. Pour over the clams or mussels and serve immediately, with *khoubz* (Arab bread) or pitta to mop up the sauce.

LEBANESE TUNA SALAD

SERVES 6–8

Although fresh tuna is available along the coast, tinned tuna is just as popular as a convenience food as it is in Britain. This version makes a delicious change from the more unusual Western tuna salads and can serve as a great filling for *khoubz* or pitta bread.

- *3 medium-sized red peppers*
- *2 garlic cloves, crushed*
- *Salt and freshly ground pepper*
- *45 ml/3 tbsp lemon juice*
- *120 ml/4 fl oz olive oil*
- *1 large red onion, finely chopped*
- *30 ml/2 tbsp finely chopped fresh coriander*
- *100 g/4 oz pitted black olives, sliced*
- *2 hard-boiled eggs, chopped*
- *2 × 200 g/7 oz tin white tuna in oil or brine*
- *Lemon wedges*

Place the 3 peppers on a rack under a hot preheated grill, and cook, turning occasionally, until the skins are charred and blackened. Remove the peppers and place them in a paper or plastic bag and leave for 15 minutes.

Meanwhile, mash the garlic in a large bowl with a little salt until you have a paste. Whisk in the lemon juice and then the olive oil in a slow stream, until the dressing is emulsified. Stir in the onion and coriander.

Remove the peppers from the bag and skin them. Core and seed them, cut away the inner ribs, then cut the flesh into short thin strips. Stir the pepper strips into the dressing, cover and chill for 1 hour.

Gently fold in the olives, chopped eggs and flaked tuna. Stir to combine. Transfer the salad to a serving platter and garnish with lemon wedges.

PISTACHIO-FRIED FISH
SAMAK BI PISTACHIO

SERVES 6

In Lebanon, the white fish used for this dish might be grouper (*merou*) or sea bream (*farrideh*). Here bream, sole or bass would do as well.

- *50 g/2 oz fine dry breadcrumbs*
- *100 g/4 oz shelled pistachios, finely chopped and crushed*
- *45 ml/3 tbsp finely chopped flat-leaved parsley*
- *Salt and freshly ground pepper*
- *2 eggs*
- *6 × 175 g/5 oz white fish fillets*
- *75 g/3 oz* semnah *or a combination of butter and olive oil*
- *Juice of 2 oranges*
- *Orange wedges*
- *Toasted chopped pistachios*

On a large plate, mix together the breadcrumbs, crushed nuts, parsley and seasoning to taste. In a shallow bowl, beat the two eggs lightly.

Dip the fish pieces, one at a time, into the egg. Drain briefly, then coat both sides in the nut mixture, patting them to ensure an even covering. Shake off any excess mixture.

Heat half of the *semnah,* or half of the butter and oil mixture, in a large frying pan. Sauté the fillets, 3 at a time, for about 5 minutes on each side, turning once with a spatula. Remove and keep warm while frying the remaining 3 fillets.

Before serving, deglaze the pan with the orange juice. Arrange the fillets on a serving platter, pour over the pan juices and serve, garnished with toasted pistachios and oranges wedges.

FISH AND RICE IN BROTH

SAYADIEH

SERVES 6

This is one of the most popular Arab fish dishes and a firm favourite of Lebanese fish restaurants. Each chef has his own particular twist – some sauté the fish first, some stew it; some purée the onions, some keep them whole; the garnishes vary as well. The following is a representative version.

- *100 g/4 oz plain flour*
- *Salt and freshly ground pepper*
- *Large pinch ground chilli pepper*
- *6 × 175 g/5 oz white fish fillets – sea bass, bream, cod or halibut*
- *250 ml/8 fl oz olive oil*
- *4 onions, chopped*
- *5 ml/1 tsp ground cumin*
- *Juice of 2 lemons*
- *450 g/1 lb long-grain rice*
- *30 ml/2 tbsp sliced blanched almonds, toasted*
- *Chopped flat-leaved parsley*

On a large plate mix together the flour, salt and pepper to taste, and a pinch of chilli; toss with the hands to combine. Dip each of the fillets in the seasoned flour, shake off excess and put aside.

Heat 45 ml/3 tbsp of the oil in a large casserole with a cover, and sauté three of the fillets for about 8–10 minutes, until just opaque, turning once. Take the fish out, add a little more oil, and cook the remaining three fillets until done. Keep all the cooked fillets warm in a very low oven, covered with foil.

Add the remaining oil to the pan, stir in the chopped onions and sauté over medium-low heat, until they are softened and very lightly coloured. Pour over 4–5 cups of water, bring to the boil, cover, and reduce the heat. Cook for about 10 minutes, until the onions are mushy. Pour the broth into a blender or food processor and purée in batches until it is smooth.

Return half the broth to the casserole, add salt to taste, the juice of 1 lemon and the rice. Add a little more water to cover, if necessary. Bring to the boil, cover and cook for a few minutes on high heat, then reduce the heat and cook for about 10 minutes over low heat. Take the rice off the heat, and allow to sit, covered, for another 10 minutes, until it is soft and fluffs with a fork.

Meanwhile put the remaining half of the onion broth in a small saucepan, add the remaining lemon juice and reduce the liquid over high heat to about half.

Transfer the rice to a heated serving dish with a rim, arranging it in a mound. Arrange the fillets around the rice, and pour over the lemon-onion broth. Sprinkle over the toasted almond slices and chopped parsley and serve immediately.

A Roman mosaic fish at Baalbek.

GRILLED SARDINES

SERVES 4

Grilled sardines are eaten in all the coastal ports of the Mediterranean, and Lebanon is no exception. The secret to their appeal is the freshness of the fish and the method of cooking – grilling over hot coals. If you do not have access to a barbecue, an oven grill is an acceptable second best.

- *8 fresh small sardines, trimmed, cleaned, de-scaled*
- *75 ml/3 fl oz olive oil*
- *Juice of 1 lemon*
- *5 ml/1 tsp ground cardamom*
- *30 ml/2 tbsp finely chopped flat-leaved parsley*
- *Salt and freshly ground pepper*
- *Lemon slices*

Wash the fish under running water, making sure all the scales have been removed. Wash the inside of the fish as well. Pat dry with absorbent paper.

In a bowl, mix together the oil, lemon juice, cardamom and chopped parsley. Spoon over the fish and rub in with the fingers. Season the dish to taste with salt and pepper.

Cook the fish under a preheated hot grill for about 3 minutes a side, basting with the flavoured oil. Grill until the skin is charred and the flesh is white, and flakes easily with a fork.

Remove to a warmed platter and pour the remaining oil over the fish. Serve garnished with lemon slices.

CHILLED CUCUMBER AND MINT SQUID

SERVES 6

Like all Mediterranean cuisines, that of Lebanon makes good use of two of the stranger denizens of the deep – octopus and squid. This is a summery salad, which can be extended with other seafood if required.

- *1.5 kg/3 lb cleaned small squid, cut into rings and strips*
- *250 ml/8 fl oz fish stock*
- *250 ml/8 fl oz dry white wine*
- *4 spring onions, finely chopped*
- *2 cucumbers, peeled, halved and seeded, and thinly sliced*
- *18 cherry tomatoes, halved*
- *Lettuce leaves*

DRESSING

- *15 ml/1 tbsp lemon juice*
- *1 garlic clove, crushed*
- *2.5 ml/½ tsp caster sugar*
- *5 ml/1 tsp Dijon mustard*
- *120 ml/4 fl oz olive oil*
- *Large pinch cayenne pepper*
- *2.5 ml/½ tsp ground cumin*
- *15 ml/1 tbsp finely chopped mint leaves*
- *250 ml/8 fl oz Greek-style yoghurt*

In a large saucepan, combine the squid, fish stock and wine. Bring to the boil, cover and simmer for about 40 minutes or until tender, stirring occasionally to move the squid pieces around. Drain the squid and pat dry. Allow to cool.

Meanwhile make the dressing. In a large bowl, whisk together the lemon juice, garlic, sugar and mustard. Slowly add the oil in a stream, whisking, until the dressing is emulsified. Beat in the cayenne to taste, ground cumin and the mint leaves. Then gently stir in the yoghurt, mixing it in thoroughly.

Add the cooled squid to the bowl and toss gently to coat in the yoghurt dressing. Chill the squid for 2–3 hours. Before serving, gently fold in the chopped spring onions, sliced cucumber and halved tomatoes, and arrange on a bed of lettuce.

FISH IN SESAME SAUCE
SAMAK BI TAHINI

SERVES 6

Tahini **(sesame seed) paste can be bought at health food shops and at most delicatessens. The sauce made with *tahini* is often called simply *taratoor*, but should not be confused with the pine nut *Taratoor* (page 104). The sesame *taratoor* used in this recipe is usually baked with fish or cauliflower.**

- *400 ml/14 fl oz* taratoor bi tahini *(page 106)*
- *120 ml/4 fl oz olive oil*
- *2 large onions, thinly sliced*
- *6 white fish fillets (bream, grouper, brill, sea bass, or suchlike)*
- *Salt and freshly ground pepper*

Make the *taratoor* first, and set it aside.

Heat the olive oil in a frying pan. Add the onions and sauté, stirring frequently, until they are limp and lightly golden.

Preheat the oven to 180°C/350°F/Gas Mark 4.

Transfer the onions to a large baking dish. Roll each of the fillets in the onions to coat with the oil, then arrange the fish on top of the onions, skin side up. Season to taste, cover with foil and bake for 15 minutes. Remove, and if desired, pass the fish under a hot grill for a few minutes to crisp the skin.

Spoon the *taratoor* sauce over the fish and onions. Return the fish to the oven at the same temperature and bake, uncovered, for a further 20–25 minutes, or until the sauce is bubbling. Serve with pilau rice.

BAKED FISH
SAMAK FILFORN

SERVES 4–6

This common Western method of baking fish has been adopted by the Lebanese with enthusiasm, since it suits much of the typical Mediterranean catch, allows spices to be rubbed into the fish, and is admirably suited to fish that are to be served cold. The last of these is a popular Lebanese treatment, with the chilled, whole fish or fillets covered in *Taratoor bi Tahini* (page 106) or *Nougada* (page 95) sauce, or served with Green Mayonnaise (page 110) or Lemon Relish (page 111).

- *Juice of ½ lemon*
- *1 garlic clove, crushed*
- *120 ml/4 fl oz olive oil*
- *10 ml/2 tsp oregano*
- *Salt and freshly ground pepper*
- *1 whole sea bass or bream, or 2–3 whole red mullet, depending on size*
- *Lemon wedges (optional)*

In a small bowl, mash the garlic into the lemon juice until you have a paste. Whisk in the olive oil, until emulsified, then the oregano and seasoning to taste.

Place the fish on a large piece of aluminium foil, and pour some of the marinade over it. Rub it into the fish on both sides. Close the foil over the fish(es), and chill for 1–2 hours.

Preheat the oven to 180°C/350°F/Gas Mark 4. Open the foil, pour over a little more marinade, and seal again. Place on a baking tray and cook for 40–50 minutes, depending on the number and size of the fish. Test by inserting a knife or skewer into the flesh; it should be opaque.

Serve hot with lemon wedges, or cold – with the skin removed – embellished with one of the above-mentioned sauces or with the sauce served alongside.

BAKED STUFFED FISH

SAMAK HARRAH

SERVES 6

This is a recipe with many variations. The optional pomegranate seeds are an introduction from Iran, but one that is much appreciated in Lebanon. If the stuffed fish is white-fleshed, it is often served cold with a *Taratoor bi Sonoba* (Pine Nut Sauce); if an oily fish, it is always served hot, without sauce, simply garnished with lemon wedges.

- *1.75 kg/4 lb sea bass or grey mullet, cleaned, gutted and scaled (or 6 × 275 g/10 oz whole mackerel)*
- *Olive oil*
- *Salt and freshly ground pepper*
- *1 small onion, finely chopped*
- *½ green pepper, finely chopped*
- *75 g/3 oz pine nuts*
- *2.5 ml/½ tsp bruised coriander seeds*
- *25 g/1 oz fresh breadcrumbs*
- *30–45 ml/2–3 tbsp sultanas*
- *30 ml/2 tbsp pomegranate seeds (optional)*
- *75 ml/5 tbsp finely chopped flat-leaved parsley*
- *60 ml/4 tbsp fresh lemon juice*
- *Cucumber, olives, tomatoes, green peppers, pimento, anchovies, hard-boiled eggs, toasted pine nuts (optional)*
- *Lemon wedges or* Taratoor bi Sonoba *(page 104; optional)*

If you are stuffing one whole white fish, rub it liberally with olive oil and rub in salt and pepper to taste. Leave to chill for 1 hour.

If using mackerel, do not let your fishmonger gut them; take them home whole. Sever the heads, leaving them attached by a small piece of skin. Snap the tail sharply, breaking the backbone inside the fish, and roll it back and forth to loosen the bone and flesh.

Using a spoon, scoop out the innards of the fish, and follow this by drawing out the loosened backbone. Use the spoon to press the flesh against the sides of the fish, enlarging the hole for stuffing. Wash the fish inside and out, pat dry and set aside.

To make the stuffing, heat 45 ml/3 tbsp olive oil. Sauté the onion for about 5 minutes over medium heat, stirring, until softened. Add the green pepper and continue stirring, until it is soft and the onions are changing colour. Stir in the pine nuts for another 2 minutes, then the crushed coriander seeds and breadcrumbs. Stir for about 1 minute. Remove the pan from the heat and add the sultanas, pomegranate seeds (if used) and the parsley. Season the stuffing with salt and pepper to taste, and moisten it with 15 ml/1 tbsp lemon juice.

Preheat the oven to 200°C/400°F/Gas Mark 6. Stuff the large white fish or the smaller mackerel with the mixture. Secure the white fish with a little thread or small skewers; fill the mackerel through the top opening and replace the heads as well as possible. Arrange the fish on a baking tray, pour over the remaining lemon juice (and more oil on the white fish, if this is necessary).

Place the fish in the preheated oven and bake, covered loosely with foil, for about 40–45 minutes for the whole fish, or about 30 for the six mackerel.

Remove from the oven. Serve the mackerel immediately with lemon wedges; the white fish may also be served hot or it may be allowed to cool and served with the *taratoor*.

In the latter case, the fish is usually garnished with paper-thin cucumber slices, olive rings, tomato roses with green pepper leaves, pimento and anchovy strips, hard-boiled egg slices and toasted pine nuts.

SARDINE-STUFFED LEMONS

HAMID MASHI WI SAERDIN

SERVES 6

Sardines, like lentils, are a traditional food of the poor, which now have considerable cachet among the foodies. Coastal Lebanon has always appreciated them, however, usually simply grilled (page 69) or stuffed and baked (see Baked Stuffed Fish, page 72). This is a different presentation, eaten as a light lunch or a European-style first course.

- *3 plump round lemons*
- *2 × 150 g/5 oz tin sardines packed in oil, drained*
- *45 ml/3 tbsp mayonnaise*
- *22 ml/1½ tbsp Dijon mustard*
- *1 large celery stalk, finely chopped*
- *4 spring onions, finely chopped*
- *30 ml/2 tbsp finely chopped flat-leaved parsley*
- *Salt and freshly ground pepper*
- *30 ml/2 tbsp pine nuts, toasted*
- *Green olives, cut lengthwise into slivers*

Halve the lemons and squeeze them with a juicer, reserve the juice. Take each half and carefully cut a thin slice from the bottom so that it will stand. With your fingers, try to remove as much as possible of the inner membrane from each half. Place the halves upside down for a few minutes.

Meanwhile decant the drained sardines into a bowl. Mash together with the mayonnaise, mustard and 30 ml/2 tbsp of the lemon juice. Try to obtain a fairly smooth paste. Work in the chopped celery, onions and parsley. Season to taste and give a final stir.

Divide the sardine paste among the six lemon halves, shape the tops attractively and garnish with a few toasted pine nuts and slivers of green olive. Chill briefly (or up to 2 hours) and serve with warm *khoubz* (Arab bread) or pitta.

FISH KEBABS

SAMAK KEBAB

SERVES 6

Kebabs are one of the most typical dishes of the Middle East. Those made with fish, however, are usually encountered only along the coast. Kebabs are usually cooked over hot coals, but these fish kebabs work well under a grill. They go well with Lemon Relish (page 110).

- *4 onions, roughly chopped*
- *Juice of 3 lemons*
- *60 ml/2 fl oz olive oil*
- *Large pinch cayenne pepper*
- *10 ml/2 tsp cumin*
- *15 ml/1 tbsp tomato purée*
- *2 bay leaves*
- *900 g/2 lb fillet of lotte or sea bass, cut into 2.5 cm/1 in cubes*
- *18–24 cherry tomatoes*
- *6 baby courgettes, trimmed, scrubbed and cut into 3–4 pieces each*
- *Olive oil*
- *Lemon wedges*

Using a garlic press, squeeze the juice from the onion pieces a little at a time, until you have extracted as much as you can. In a bowl mix the onion juice with the lemon juice and whisk in the oil, cayenne to taste, cumin and tomato purée. Add the bay leaves.

Place the cubed fish in a larger bowl and pour the marinade over it; toss the fish using the hands. Cover and leave to chill for 1 hour.

On 6 large or 12 small skewers, thread the fish cubes, baby courgettes and cherry tomatoes. Place over hot coals or under a preheated hot grill, and brush with a little oil, especially on the vegetables. Cook for about 10–15 minutes, turning once or twice, until the fish is opaque and the courgettes are just tender. Serve immediately with lemon wedges and rice or burghul.

POULTRY AND EGGS
TOUYOUR WI BEID

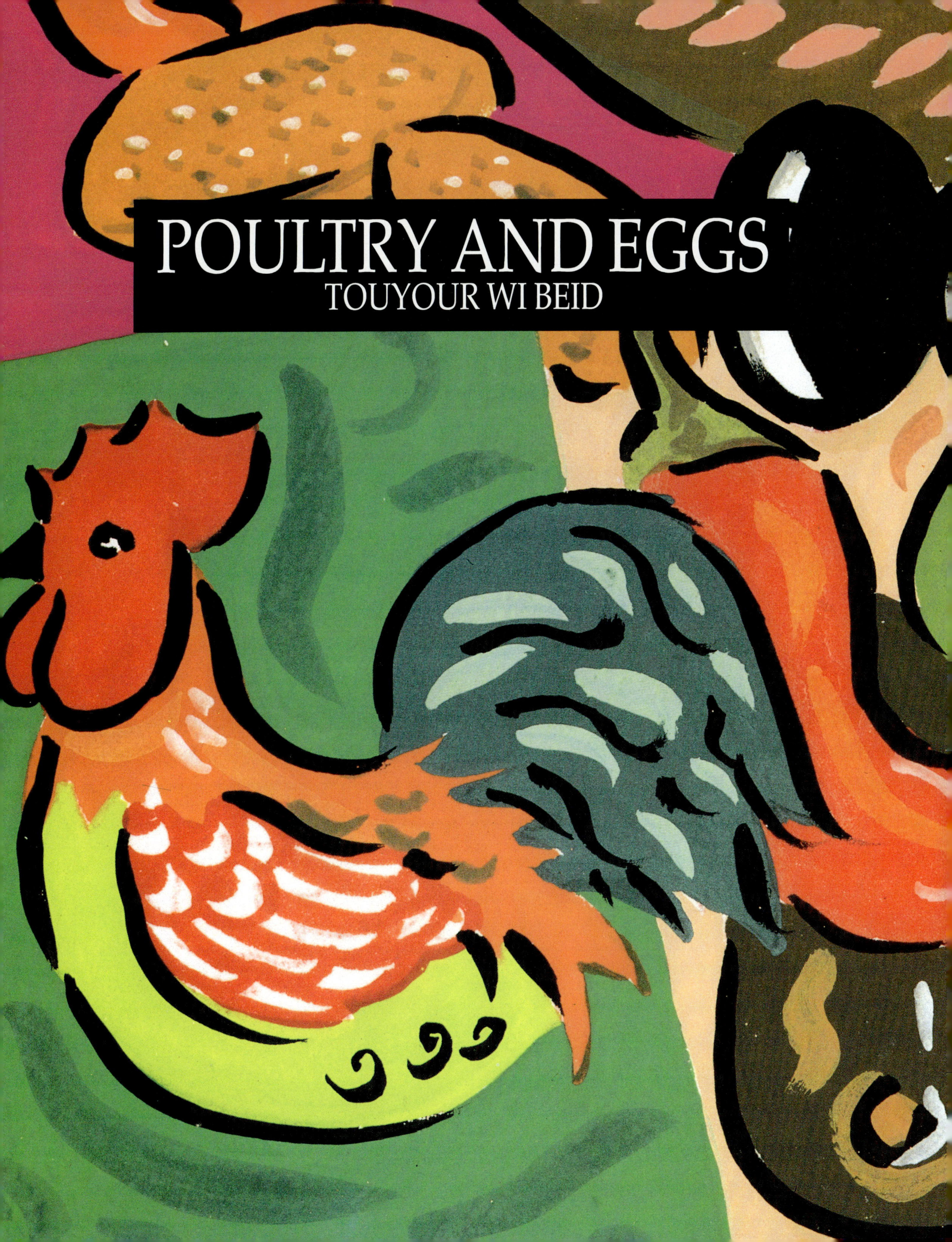

GRILLED GARLIC CHICKEN
FARROUGE MISHWA

SERVES 4–6

This treatment is particularly good with whole poussins, split in half, flattened with a mallet and rubbed with paprika, then submerged in the marinade. It can also be made with tender chicken pieces.

- *3 x 675 g/1½ lb poussins, halved and flattened, or 6–8 chicken pieces*
- *15 ml/1 tbsp paprika*
- *Salt and freshly ground pepper*
- *60 ml/4 tbsp* Taratoor bi Sade *(page 111) or 3 garlic cloves, crushed*
- *45 ml/3 tbsp olive oil*
- *30–60 ml/2–4 tbsp lemon juice*
- *Fresh watercress*
- *Lemon quarters*

Rub the flattened chicken halves or pieces with the paprika and salt and pepper, making sure that the spices are well distributed. In a small bowl, whisk together the *taratoor*, olive oil and 30 ml/2 tbsp lemon juice. (Alternatively, if no *taratoor* is available, mash the garlic with the oil, then whisk in 60 ml/4 tbsp lemon juice.)

Pour the marinade over the chicken, turning the pieces in it. If necessary, add a little more oil. Cover and chill overnight.

Grill the poussin halves or chicken pieces over hot coals, which are whitening with ash. Turn 3 or 4 times, until browned and lightly charred on the outside, but succulent within. This will take 20–40 minutes, depending on the size of the pieces. Check by inserting a skewer into a meaty part; the juice should run clear. (Alternatively, cook under a preheated oven grill, turning occasionally, until done.)

Serve the chicken hot, on a bed of watercress with lemon quarters for squeezing over.

GARLIC CHICKEN WINGS
JAWANEH

SERVES 6

The method of marinating and cooking these wings is very like *Farrouge Mishwa* (page 76). However, chicken wings are a particular favourite of the Lebanese, often served as a *meze*, and therefore deserve a name of their own.

- *12–18 chicken wings, tips trimmed off*
- *10 ml/2 tsp paprika*
- *5 ml/1 tsp ground cumin*
- *3–4 garlic cloves, crushed*
- *Salt and freshly ground pepper*
- *Juice of 1 lemon*
- *60–75 ml/4–5 tbsp olive oil*
- *120 ml/4 fl oz* Taratoor bi Tahini *(page 106)*

Wash the chicken wings and pat dry. Rub in the paprika and cumin with your hands. In a small bowl, mash the garlic cloves with salt and pepper to taste, then whisk in the lemon juice and oil until combined. Pour over the chicken wings in a shallow dish, turning to coat them.

Cook the wings for about 20 minutes over hot coals, which have turned grey, turning and basting the wings with the marinade until they are tender, but cooked inside and golden brown and slightly charred outside. (Alternatively, cook under a medium-hot preheated grill, turning occasionally, until done.)

Spoon a little *taratoor bi tahini* in a strip down each wing and serve piping hot.

LEBANESE STUFFED CHICKEN
DAJAJ MASHI

SERVES 6

Stuffed poultry is a favourite all over the Arab world, from Morocco – where stuffing made with couscous, cinnamon and pickled lemon pieces – to Lebanon and Syria, where the staple ingredient varies between burghul and rice, both of which are usually enriched with nuts and herbs.

- *60 g/4 tbsp* semnah *or butter*
- *225 g/8 oz ground lamb*
- *1 large onion, finely chopped*
- *30 ml/2 tbsp pine nuts*
- *15 ml/1 tbsp raisins*
- *225 g/8 oz long-grain rice*
- *Salt and freshly ground black pepper*
- *2 kg/4½ lb free-range roasting chicken*
- *45 ml/3 tbsp Greek-style yoghurt*
- *15 ml/1 tbsp honey*

Heat 15 ml/1 tbsp butter in a frying pan. Gently sauté the ground lamb, stirring to ensure it browns all over. Transfer the meat with a slotted spoon to a plate, add another 15 ml/1 tbsp butter to the pan and stir in the finely chopped onion. Sauté over medium-low heat for about 5 minutes, until it is limp; add the pine nuts and continue to sauté until both onions and nuts are lightly coloured. Add the raisins and rice, and stir for a minute or two until the rice is transparent: season to taste. Pour in 475 ml/1 pint water and bring to the boil. Reduce the heat, cover and simmer for about 25 minutes, or until the rice has absorbed all the water. Leave until it is cool enough to handle.

Preheat the oven to 200°C/400°F/Gas Mark 6. Melt the remaining *semnah* or butter in a saucepan, take off the heat; stir in the honey until it melts, then the yoghurt. Stuff the chicken with the rice mixture, and secure the opening with skewers. Leave the remaining rice in the pan to be warmed up later. Place the chicken in a roasting pan and baste generously with the yoghurt sauce.

Roast for 20 minutes at the above temperature, then reduce the heat to 180°C/350°F/Gas Mark 4 for a further 1¼–1½ hours. Baste twice with the yoghurt sauce. Test to see if the chicken is cooked by piercing the joint between body and thigh with a skewer; the juice should run clear.

Heat the remaining rice gently over low heat and moistened with a little of the chicken pan juices. Serve with the hot stuffed chicken.

Lemons flourish in the Lebanese climate.

CHICKEN WITH APRICOTS AND OLIVES

SERVES 8

This savoury combination owes more to the Israeli taste than to classic Lebanese cuisine. Israel is Europe's richest source of dried fruits, and they make a frequent appearance in the meat stews and desserts of that country. However, taste cannot be confined by national borders, and dishes like this one have become common in Lebanon, adapted to include specialities such as *arak*.

- *1.5 kg/3½ lb skinned, boned and cubed chicken*
- *5 garlic cloves, crushed*
- *100 g/4 oz chopped ready-to-eat dried apricots*
- *75 g/3 oz black Greek olives*
- *2.5 ml/½ tsp grated orange peel*
- *75 ml/5 tbsp orange juice*
- *60 ml/2 tbsp lemon juice or white wine vinegar*
- *120 ml/4 fl oz* arak *(anise-based Lebanese liqueur) or ouzo*
- *30 ml/2 tbsp fresh fennel leaves*
- *22 ml/1½ tbsp olive oil*
- *100 g/4 oz light brown sugar*

Preheat the oven to 200°C/400°F/Gas Mark 6.

Combine all the ingredients in a large bowl and stir carefully to mix well. Cover and chill overnight.

Transfer the chicken pieces to a baking tray and pour over the marinade, including the olives and apricots. Sprinkle over the sugar. Bake for about 30 minutes, turning once or twice.

Remove the chicken pieces to a serving platter, and arrange the olives and apricots over and around them. Strain the cooking juices into a saucepan, and reduce over high heat to about half. Pour the sauce over the chicken. Serve warm or cold.

MUSCAT BAKED ALMOND CHICKEN

SERVES 6

This dish is made with the sweet white-green grapes that have been grown around Cyprus and the Levant since Crusader times. Both a wine-making and a dessert grape, the muscat gives a pungent flavour and aroma to this recipe, which has its roots in a centuries-old tradition of using ground almonds as a thickening agent. In Lebanon, the herbs used would be wild – the marjoram, in particular, of a type found only in the eastern Mediterranean.

- *2 kg/4½ free-range chicken*
- *Salt and freshly ground pepper*
- *2.5 ml/½ tsp cinnamon*
- *Large pinch nutmeg*
- *Fresh lemon thyme*
- *Fresh marjoram*
- *225 g/8 oz muscat grapes, skinned, seeded and halved*
- *250 ml/8 fl oz sweet muscat wine*
- *15 ml 1 tbsp* semnah *or butter*
- *45 ml/3 tbsp sliced blanched almonds*
- *50 g/2 oz ground almonds*
- *Salt and freshly ground pepper*
- *150 ml/¼ pint single cream*
- *2 egg yolks*

Wash and pat dry the chicken, rub it all over with salt and pepper to taste, the cinnamon and the nutmeg. Take 2–3 springs of lemon thyme and the same of marjoram and put them inside the chicken. Place it in a casserole, stuff with half the grapes and pour over the wine. Cover and cook the chicken in a preheated 200°C/400°F/Gas Mark 6 oven for 1½ hours.

Remove the chicken from the oven and transfer it to a warm serving platter. Remove the grapes and herbs from the cavity, joint the chicken and cover it with foil to keep it warm.

In a small saucepan, melt the *semnah* or butter and sauté the sliced almonds for a few minutes until just coloured. Remove with a slotted spoon and set aside. Skim the fat from the chicken cooking juices in the casserole and strain them into the saucepan. Heat the juices gently until very hot, but not boiling, and stir in the remaining grapes and the ground almonds. Allow to cook for a few minutes to combine.

In a small bowl beat the cream and egg yolks together lightly. Take a spoonful of the hot chicken stock and stir it into the egg. Remove the saucepan from the heat and stir in the egg mixture; the sauce should thicken as your stir.

Pour some of the sauce over the jointed chicken and sprinkle it with the toasted almonds. Pour the remainder into a sauceboat to be served with *Mudardara* (page 98) or pilau rice.

CHEESE-FRIED EGGS

BEID BI GEBNA

SERVES 4

This dish is simplicity itself and combines two favourite Lebanese fried foods: eggs and cheese. The cheeses most usually used in Lebanon are versions of Kaseri or Halloumi; both are available from Greek, Turkish and Lebanese delicatessens in the West. Italian *pecorino* or one of the new hard English goat or ewe cheeses would make an authentically strong-tasting substitute.

- *2.5 ml/½ tsp ground cumin*
- *2.5 ml/½ tsp salt*
- *30 ml/2 tbsp* semnah *or butter*
- *4 thick slices hard cheese*
- *4 eggs*

In a small salt-cellar or egg cup, mix together the salt and cumin. Reserve.

Heat the *semnah* or butter over medium heat. Add the four cheese slices and fry for about 3 minutes, or until they begin to bubble. Crack an egg over each slice, cover and cook gently, until the egg is just done. Lift the eggy cheeses out with a spatula and serve. Offer the cumin salt; take a pinch and sprinkle over the egg before eating.

ONION-FLAVOURED HARD-BOILED EGGS

BEID HAMID

SERVES 6

These hard-boiled eggs are a Middle-Eastern favourite, with a quite distinctive flavour and a beige-brown colour when peeled. They are a delicious foil to stews, such as *Bamia* (page 91), are occasionally served quartered as *mezze*, and make a fine snack with a salad, such as *Bazinjan Rahib* (page 59).

- *6 eggs*
- *Skins from 6 onions (reserve the onions for another use)*
- *Seasoned salt and/or lemon pepper (can be bought prepared in certain shops and delicatessens)*

Place the eggs in a saucepan and cover with the onion skins. Pour in enough cold water to cover and turn the flame as low as possible. Simmer very gently for about 6–7 hours, topping up the water when necessary. (Putting a layer of oil over the water will retard evaporation, but it must still be checked occasionally.)

When the time is up, plunge the eggs into cold water and leave to cool before peeling. Serve with the seasoned salt and/or pepper, as desired. The eggs can be kept refrigerated for up to 2 days without losing their flavour.

BRAISED DUCK WITH SWEET POTATOES

SERVES 6

Live ducks as well as chickens are common denizens of Lebanese street markets, and in smaller towns such feathered livestock will be found wandering the back roads around peasant houses. The sweet potato is an introduction from Central Africa, which has been accepted into the regional cuisine and into this Maronite recipe.

- *6 duck quarters, washed and patted dry*
- *Salt and freshly ground pepper*
- *2 carrots, chopped*
- *2 celery stalks, chopped*
- *1 large onion, chopped*
- *1 garlic clove, crushed*
- *1 bay leaf*
- *5 ml/1 tsp thyme*
- *6 cardamom pods*
- *15 ml/1 tbsp tomato paste*
- *450 ml/16 fl oz duck or chicken consommé*
- *15 ml/1 tbsp olive oil*
- *4 medium sweet potatoes, peeled and roughly cubed*
- *45 ml/2 tbsp caster sugar*
- *60 ml/4 tbsp red wine vinegar*
- *15 ml/1 tbsp honey*
- *30 ml/2 tbsp sultanas*

Trim the duck of all extra skin and fat. Place the trimmings in a large shallow casserole, together with the duck quarters, seasoned with salt and pepper, and fry for about 20 minutes, until the trimmings are frizzled and the duck quarters are crisp and brown. Discard the trimmings, reserve the duck quarters, and strain the fat into a heavy saucepan.

Sauté the carrots, celery and onion in the saucepan for about 8 minutes, stirring until they are coloured and the onion is limp. Pour off the fat, stir in the garlic briefly over the heat, and add the bay leaf, thyme, cardamom, tomato paste, consommé and 250 ml/8 fl oz water. Stir to combine, bring to the boil, lower the heat slightly and simmer for 30 minutes, skimming once or twice.

Preheat the oven to 180°C/350°F/Gas Mark 4.

Place the duck back in the casserole, strain over the stock, cover and cook for about 40 minutes, or until the duck is done.

Meanwhile, put the sweet potatoes into the saucepan. Cover with water and bring to the boil. Cook for 5 minutes, then drain thoroughly. Reserve.

When the duck is cooked, remove the pieces from the casserole with a slotted spoon and strain off the juice into a bowl or fat separator. Add the olive oil to the casserole and sauté the drained sweet potatoes, stirring gently to coat all the sides, for about 5 minutes. Add the duck quarters and remove from the heat.

Skim the fat from the reserved duck stock. In a saucepan, cook the sugar and vinegar together, stirring until the mixture is beginning to caramelize. Whisk in the duck stock and honey until smooth.

Pour the sweet-sour sauce over the sweet potatoes and duck quarters, add the sultanas, and cover the casserole. Simmer for about 10 minutes. Serve immediately from the casserole.

SOUR ORANGE TURKEY
HABISH WI LAEMON

SERVES 8

The turkeys that roam unfettered in the Levant are a small black-necked breed, tasty but not always tender. This sour marinade tenderizes the meat while lending a tangy fruitiness. Sour oranges were brought to southern Europe by the Arabs, where they became better known as "Seville oranges".

- *4.5–5.5 kg/10–12 lb turkey*
- *6 sour (Seville) oranges*
- *4 garlic cloves, cut into slivers*
- *3 red or mild yellow onions*
- *30 ml/2 tbsp fresh marjoram, finely chopped*
- *60 ml/2 fl oz olive oil*
- *5 ml/1 tsp ground coriander*
- *Salt and freshly ground pepper*
- *Flat-leaved parsley*
- *150 ml/¼ pint Greek-style yoghurt (optional)*

Wash the turkey and pat it dry with absorbent paper. Squeeze the juice from 4 oranges; reserve the other 2 for the moment.

Make small gashes through the turkey skin into the flesh, and insert the garlic slivers into them. Slice two of the onions thinly into a large ceramic or enamel-lined casserole, and place the turkey on top. Scatter the marjoram on top, and pour over the orange juice. Cover the bowl and chill for 1 day, turning the turkey several times in the marinade.

Preheat the oven to 200°C/400°F/Gas Mark 6.

Take the turkey from the marinade and pat it dry. Rub all over with the olive oil, ground coriander, and salt and pepper to taste. Remove the sliced onions from the marinade with a slotted spoon and arrange them over the bottom of a baking pan. Place the turkey on top, breast side down, and pour over the marinade. Roast in the oven for 10 minutes, then lower the heat to 170°C/325°F/Gas Mark 3, and continue roasting, basting with the pan juices occasionally, for a further 2½ hours, or until the juices run clear when the turkey is pierced with a skewer or sharp knife. If necessary, add some water to the liquid to keep it from drying out.

Remove the bird from the oven, place on a serving platter, and let it rest, covered, for 15 minutes. Strain the pan juices into a saucepan. Peel the two remaining oranges, separate them into segments, and add to the saucepan. Reduce the sauce over high heat until it thickens slightly. Cut the turkey meat into serving pieces, slice the breast and arrange on the serving platter. Slice the last onion and arrange the rings over the turkey pieces. Strain over the reduced juices and orange segments. Garnish with flat-leaved parsley and serve immediately.

The turkey may also be served cold. Whisk some of the reduced juices and finely-chopped parsley into the yoghurt before chilling it.

MEAT-BASED MAIN COURSES

AL-LAHEM

LEBANESE SHISH KEBAB
LAHEM MESHWI

SERVES 6

"Shish kebab" probably originated in Turkey, but its popularity has carried the skewered meat, in various forms, as far east as Thailand, as far west as the United States and as far north as Russia. The Levantine version is made with mutton or lamb; beef or liver can be substituted by the less orthodox. The vinaigrette-like marinade is an essential.

- *900 g/2 lb tender lamb, leg or tenderloin, cut into 5 cm/2 in cubes*
- *1 large onion, quartered*
- *1 large sweet green pepper, cored and seeded*
- *18 cherry tomatoes, stems removed*

MARINADE

- *1 onion, finely sliced*
- *30 ml/2 tbsp olive oil*
- *45 ml/3 tbsp fresh lemon juice*
- *Salt and freshly ground pepper*
- *5 ml/1 tsp* Taratoor bi Sade *or 2 garlic cloves, crushed*
- *1 dried red pepper, crushed (optional)*
- *5 ml/1 tsp ground cumin*
- *½ tsp/2.5 ml/½ tsp ground cinnamon*
- *Lemon quarters*

Make the marinade first. Place the finely sliced onion in a large bowl. In a screw-top bottle, put together the other marinade ingredients (be more generous with the salt than you might normally be), cover and shake it vigorously to combine.

Put the lamb cubes (or other chosen meat) into the bowl, and pour over the marinade. Use your hands to toss the onion, meat and marinade, so that everything is coated and well mixed. Cover the bowl and chill for at least 8 hours or as long as 24.

Cut each onion quarter in half and separate each of the 8 onion sections into 3 parts, so that you have 24 onion sections. Cut the green pepper into 18 square-ish pieces. Remove the meat from the refrigerator.

Thread the pepper, meat, onion and tomatoes onto 6 large skewers, alternating the ingredients, but beginning and ending each skewer with green pepper.

Over grey-ashed charcoal, grill the kebabs for about 12–15 minutes, basting with the marinade and turning two or three times, until they are browned on the outside, but pink within. (Alternatively, cook on a rack under a preheated grill, with a tray to catch the juices.) Serve the kebabs with rice and garnish generously with lemon quarters.

ARMENIAN BAKED MINCEMEAT

KOFTA BI SAYNIYEH

SERVES 6–8

Variations of these minced lamb "sausages" are encountered in the northeastern regions, influenced by Armenian and Syrian peoples, and are also popular among Lebanese immigrants in the United States and Europe. Shaped into small balls, they can be coated in flour and deep-fried; in this recipe they are baked in tomato sauce.

- *450 g/1 lb potatoes, peeled and quartered*
- *1 onion, chopped*
- *675 g/1½ lb minced lamb or beef*
- *2 eggs*
- *60 ml/4 tbsp chopped parsley*
- *10 ml/5 tsp fried mint*
- *5 ml/1 tsp ground allspice*
- *Salt and freshly ground pepper*
- *75 ml/5 tbsp* samneh *or butter*
- *75 ml/5 tbsp pine nuts*
- *30 ml/2 tbsp tomato purée*
- *Red and yellow sweet pepper rings*
- *Lemon wedges*

Boil the potatoes until tender and then drain thoroughly. Put them into the bowl of a food processor fitted with a metal blade, together with the onion, and process until puréed. Add the minced meat, and process until the mixture is combined and of a paste-like consistency; add the eggs, herbs and spices, and season to taste. Process until all is combined, stopping the machine to scrape down the sides of the bowl once or twice. Chill the mixture for 1 hour.

Sauté the pine nuts in 20 ml/2 tbsp butter over medium heat until they are golden; cool slightly. Take the meat from the refrigerator and divide it into 8 balls. Place a sheet of greaseproof paper on a flat kitchen surface or a board, and flatten a ball into a longish rectangle. Place about 12 ml/¾ tbsp pine nuts down the centre of the rectangle, and roll the meat into a cylinder or "sausage" around it, sealing the ends. Repeat with the remaining meatballs and pine nuts.

Preheat the oven to 180°C/350°F/Gas Mark 4.

Place the 8 cylinders close together on an oiled baking tray. In a small saucepan, melt the remaining *samneh* or butter and stir in the tomato paste, beating until combined. Pour the tomato butter over the meat, making sure to cover as much of the meat as possible. Bake for about 45–50 minutes, or until the *kofas* are browned and the sauce baked in.

Served garnished with red and yellow pepper rings and lemon wedges.

TRAY KIBBEH

KIBBEH BI SAYNIYEH

Although individual *kibbeh* (page 43) are more commonly served as *mezze*, this tray *kibbeh* can also be divided into small squares for hors-d'oeuvres. But it makes a delicious main course, its somewhat dry consistency well-complemented by *Bazinjan Rahib* (page 59), served at room temperature.

- *120 ml/4 fl oz water*
- *120 ml/r fl oz tinned tomato juice*
- *60 ml/2 fl oz fresh lemon juice*
- *275 g/10 oz fine-ground burghul*
- *450 g/1 lb minced lamb*
- *5 ml/1 tsp paprika*
- *2.5 ml/½ tsp ground cumin*
- *Large pinch cayenne*
- *Salt and freshly ground pepper*
- *20 ml/1½ tbsp sesame seeds (optional)*
- *60 ml/2 fl oz melted* samneh *or butter*
- *30 ml/2 tbsp sunflower oil*

FILLING

- *15 ml/1 tbsp olive oil*
- *1 onion, finely chopped*
- *350 g/12 oz minced lamb*
- *50 g/2 oz chopped walnuts or pine nuts*
- *2.5 ml/½ tsp allspice*
- *Salt and freshly ground pepper*

Make the *kibbeh* "pastry". In a bowl, stir together the water, tomato juice and lemon juice. Add the burghul, mix in and allow to rest for 10 minutes.

In the bowl of a food processor, combine the minced lamb, spices and salt and pepper to taste; process until the meat has been ground into a more paste-like consistency. Add the burghul and juice with the motor running, little by little, until it is combined thoroughly.

Remove the meat paste to a bowl and squeeze with the hands until it has a more elastic feel, then chill for 2 hours.

Meanwhile make the filling. In a frying pan, heat the olive oil, and sauté the onion in it until it is limp and lightly coloured. Add the minced lamb and cook, stirring, until the meat is browned. Take off the heat, drain off the excess fat and stir in the nuts, allspice and seasoning to taste.

Mix together the melted *semneh* or butter and the sunflower oil. Brush a little over the bottom of a square baking tin. Divide the chilled *kibbeh* "pastry" in half. Take small handfuls from one half and flatten between moistened hands. Press the pieces into the base of the tin, joining them up to form a bottom crust. Spoon in the filling, spreading it evenly over the *kibbeh*. Take more small handfuls from the second half of the *kibbeh* and make the top crust to go over the filling. Pat it on evenly up to the edges of the tin. Pat the sesame seeds, if used, into the crust.

Preheat the oven to 200°C/400°F/Gas Mark 6.

Divide the "pie" into serving pieces with a sharp knife – either large squares for a main course or small diamonds for a *mezze*. Brush with the *samneh* and oil mixture, allowing it to sink into the divisions. Bake the tray *kibbeh* for 10 minutes, then lower the heat to 180°/350°F/Gas Mark 4, and bake for a further 30–35 minutes. Remove from the oven and allow to cool slightly before lifting the slices. Serve with Yoghurt and Cucumber Sauce (page 108), if desired.

The tray *kibbeh* can also be chilled and served cold.

Flowers growing above lake Qaraoun.

LIVER WITH MINT
KIBDEH BI NA'NA

SERVES 4

This is an unusual combination of flavours to Western tastes, but is exquisite. If fresh mint is not available, half the quantity of dried mint can be used, although the result will not be as subtle – or as visually attractive.

- *30 ml/2 tbsp* samneh *or combination of butter and olive oil*
- *1 onion, finely sliced*
- *1 garlic clove, crushed*
- *450 g/1 lb calves' or lambs' liver, very thinly sliced*
- *Flour for dredging*
- *120 ml/4 fl oz red wine vinegar*
- *30 ml/2 tbsp very finely chopped fresh mint*

Heat 30 ml/2 tbsp *samneh* or the butter and oil over medium-high heat. Sauté the onion until it is limp, add the garlic and continue cooking until the onion is lightly coloured. Remove the onion and garlic with a slotted spoon and reserve.

Quickly dredge the liver in the flour and shake off the excess. Add the remaining *samneh* or butter/oil to the pan and sauté the liver slices quickly on both sides. Return the onions and garlic to the pan, pour in the vinegar, and stir in the mint. Cook for about 5 minutes, spooning the sauce over the liver, until the liquid is reduced and glazes the meat.

LAMB KNUCKLE STEW
LAHMA BI HOUMUS WI TOMATIM

SERVES 4

Lamb knuckle is familiar to Western foodies as the main ingredient of that Greek taverna staple Lamb Kleftiko. It is an economical dish in any guise; in Lebanon it is often stewed with green beans, or as here, with chickpeas.

- *15 ml/1 tbsp olive oil*
- *2 onions, sliced*
- *3 garlic cloves, finely chopped*
- *5 ml/1 tsp allspice*
- *10 ml/2 tsp ground cumin*
- *Pinch crushed dried red pepper flakes*
- *1 bay leaf, crushed*
- *4 meaty knuckles of lamb (about 350 g/12 oz each)*
- *2 x 400 g/14 oz cans chickpeas, drained and rinsed*
- *2 x 400 g/14 oz tin chopped tomatoes*
- *475 ml/16 fl oz lamb or beef stock*
- *Salt and freshly ground pepper*
- *1 lemon*
- *50 g/2 oz chopped coriander*

Preheat the oven to 220°C/475°F/Gas Mark 7.

Pour the oil into a casserole in which the knuckles will fit in one layer with space to spare. Heat over medium heat, add the sliced onion and sauté for 4 minutes, then add the garlic and continue cooking until the onion and garlic are limp and lightly coloured, about 6 minutes.

Remove the hot onions with a slotted spoon to a large bowl, stir in the spices and bay leaf, and reserve. Add the knuckles to the casserole, turning in the oil to brown them. Transfer the casseroled lamb to the oven, and bake for 35 minutes, turning the knuckles occasionally.

Add the chickpeas, tomatoes and stock to the onions in the bowl and mix together. Remove the casserole from the oven, pour the chickpea and tomato mixture over the knuckles and season to taste. Bring the stew to the boil on top of the stove, then cover and continue baking for another hour on the lower shelf of the oven. Test the knuckle with a knife for doneness; it should pierce easily.

Squeeze the juice from the lemon and sprinkle the coriander over the stew. Serve immediately.

STEWED MEAT AND OKRA

BAMIA MASLU

SERVES 4–6

For a change, this dish is usually made with beef, although lamb may also be used. The okra does not have to be parboiled, but if it is not it has a rather glutinous consistency – a trait not despised by the Lebanese, but generally rather disliked in the West. The choice is yours.

- *900 g/2 lb okra (ladies' fingers)*
- *60 ml/4 tbsp* samneh *or combination of butter and olive oil*
- *2 onions, finely sliced*
- *1 garlic clove, crushed*
- *675 g/1½ lb lean braising beef, cut into 2.5 cm/1 in cubes*
- *45 ml/3 tbsp tomato purée*
- *350 ml/12 fl oz hot beef stock*
- *Salt and freshly ground pepper*
- *30 ml/2 tbsp red wine vinegar or lemon juice*
- *30 ml/2 tbsp finely chopped coriander*

Trim the stems off the okra. (If you are very careful, and manage to trim the stems without cutting into the inner ribbed section of the okra, it will not bleed on cooking, and you can avoid parboiling.) Bring a large saucepan of water to the boil. Drop in the trimmed okra, bring back to the boil, and cook for 3 minutes. Drain thoroughly.

Heat 45 ml/3 tbsp of the *samneh* or butter and oil in a flameproof casserole, and sauté the onion over medium heat for 5 minutes, or until limp. Add the garlic and continue to cook for another few minutes, until the onion is lightly coloured. Remove the onion with a slotted spoon and add the last 15 ml/1 tbsp *samneh* and the meat. Sauté, turning and stirring, until the meat is browned all over. Add the drained okra and fry for about 3 more minutes, then return the onions to the casserole.

Stir the tomato purée into the heated beef stock, and pour the liquid over the meat and vegetables. Bring back to the boil, cover and lower the heat. Simmer, stirring occasionally, for about 1 hour 45 minutes, or until the meat is very tender when pierced. Top up the liquid with a little water during cooking, if necessary. Just before serving, stir in 30 ml/2 tbsp red wine vinegar or lemon juice and the chopped coriander. Serve immediately.

STUFFED COURGETTES
KOUSA MASHI

SERVES 4

This dish is usually made with minced lamb, but it can be varied with beef. For the vegetable, aubergines or any small squash can be used. The Lebanese and Syrians use a special vegetable corer, called a *munara,* to make this dish. An apple corer, knife or a small melon baller will do as well.

- *30 ml/2 tbsp olive oil*
- *1 onion, finely chopped*
- *1 garlic clove, finely chopped*
- *50 g/2 oz raisins*
- *100 g/4 oz uncooked long-grain rice*
- *5 ml/1 tsp dried mint*
- *1 tsp Lebanese spice (page 16)*
- *225 g/8 oz minced lean lamb*
- *4 medium-sized courgettes (about 18 cm/7 in long and 4 cm/1½ in diameter)*
- *Salt and freshly ground pepper*
- *750 ml/1¼ pints lamb or beef stock*
- *Fresh mint leaves*
- *Fresh yellow courgette blossoms (optional)*

Heat the olive oil in a saucepan. Sauté the onion for 6 minutes, until limp, then add the garlic and continue cooking until they are both lightly coloured. Remove from the heat and stir in the raisins, rice, mint and spice. Allow to cool slightly.

Meanwhile, core the courgettes. Cut off the stem ends and carefully hollow out each courgette, leaving a thin (3mm/⅛ in) shell. Set aside.

Scrape the rice mixture into the bowl of a food processor fitted with a metal blade. Process very briefly to chop the ingredients coarsely. Return to the saucepan or a bowl. Put the minced lamb into the processor and run the machine, pulsing and stopping to scrape down the sides, until the meat is a fine paste. Add the meat to the rice mixture and knead the two together until smooth.

Using your fingers and a long-handled spoon, carefully stuff each courgette with some of the meat mixture, filling it as tightly as possible.

Pour the stock into a shallow casserole or flameproof baking dish with a lid. Add the courgettes, season to taste, and cover. Bring to the boil, then lower the heat and simmer for about 25 minutes, or until the courgettes are tender.

Transfer the courgettes to a serving platter, and garnish with fresh mint leaves and courgette blossoms, if available. Serve the stuffed courgettes with the reduced stock or with Yoghurt and Cucumber Sauce (page 108).

A vineyard in the Bekkah valley.

MINCE KEBABS
KOFTA HALAKUYEH

SERVES 6–8

Variations of mince "rolls" are found all over the Middle East, Greece, Turkey and the Balkan states, and are well-known in the West from their frequent appearance on "kebab house" menus. What distinguishes the national versions are the spicing and special ingredients and, as in the Armenian *Kofta* (page 87), the method of cooking. This Lebanese recipe is satisfying but simple.

- *4 slices bread, crusts removed and cubed (about 175 g/5 oz)*
- *1 garlic clove, crushed*
- *900 g/2 lb minced lamb*
- *2 small onions, grated*
- *7.5 ml/1½ oz ground cumin*
- *2.5 ml/½ tsp cayenne*
- *45 ml/3 tbsp finely chopped parsley*
- *1 egg*
- *Salt and freshly ground pepper*
- *Lemon wedges*

Place the bread cubes in a small bowl and add enough water to dampen them – about 60–75 ml/4–5 tbsp. Add the garlic and, with the hands, mash the bread and garlic with the water. Leave to stand for about 10 minutes.

In a large bowl, mix together the minced lamb, grated onion, cumin, cayenne and parsley. Work with the hands to combine. Knead in the bread paste, the egg and seasoning to taste, until everything is mixed and the meat has absorbed the liquid and become drier and smoother.

With the hands, roll the meat into 6–8, long cylinders. Pass a skewer through each cylinder and pat the meat around to secure it.

Cook the kebabs over grey-ashed coals for about 20 minutes, until they are brown on all sides. (Alternatively, cook under a hot grill, turning two or three times, until done.)

Serve the kebabs with the lemon wedges and with *Caçik* (page 59), if desired.

SPICED LAMB CHOPS
KASTALETA GHANAM

SERVES 6

These spiced chops bear more than a passing resemblance to the lamb tandoori dishes of India, and show how influences have passed from one part of the Muslim world to another.

- *120 ml/4 fl oz* samneh *or butter*
- *2.5 ml/½ tsp* Lebanese spice *(page 16)*
- *1.5 ml/1¼ tsp ground cardamom*
- *4 ml/¾ tsp ground ginger*
- *1.5 ml/¼ tsp ground nutmeg*
- *Large pinch of coriander*
- *Pinch of cloves*
- *15 ml/1 tbsp freshly chopped mint*
- *15 ml/1 tbsp freshly chopped flat-leaved parsley*
- *7.5 ml/1½ tsp* Taratoor bi Sade *(page 111) or 1 garlic clove, crushed*
- *Salt and freshly ground pepper*
- *12 trimmed loin lamb chops*

In a small saucepan, slowly melt the *samneh* or butter over low heat. Add all the spices, the mint and the parsley, stir once or twice, then remove from the heat. Stir in the *taratoor* (or crushed garlic) and leave for at least 1 hour at room temperature to allow all of the flavours to mingle.

Season the lamb chops with salt and pepper to taste. Melt the seasoned *samneh*, if it has congealed, and brush the meat with it. Cook the chops over grey-ashed coals or under a preheated grill for about 6–8 minutes a side, until the outside is well-browned but the inside is still pink. Transfer the chops to serving plates and pour over the remaining seasoned *samneh* or butter. This goes well with *Imjadra* (page 98) or *Batatas bi Houmus* (page 100).

GRAINS AND VEGETABLES
KHUDRAWAT, ROZ WI BURGHUL

COURGETTES WITH WALNUTS
KOUSA IN GAMAEL

SERVES 4–6

Although walnuts appear less in Lebanese recipes than pine nuts and pistachios – walnuts are more usually associated with Turkish cuisine – they are still a valued ingredient in many dishes, both desserts and savouries.

- *60 g/5 tbsp butter or olive oil*
- *675 g/1½ lb courgettes, washed, trimmed and thinly sliced*
- *Salt and freshly ground black pepper*
- *75 g/3 oz walnut halves, chopped*
- *Large pinch of allspice*
- *30 ml/2 tbsp finely chopped parsley*

Heat the oil in a heavy frying pan and sauté the courgettes, stirring them, for about 5 minutes, or until soft. Season with salt and pepper, then stir in the walnuts and allspice. Combine well, take off the heat and scatter the parsley on top. Serve immediately.

PASTA WITH LEMON AND OIL

MACARONA BI LAEMON

SERVES 4–6

Recipes for a simple type of pasta can be found in old Arab recipe books, although there was never much traditional use of pasta in Lebanon. However, macaroni, tagliatelle and other Italian-style durum-wheat pastas have now become widespread there – treated with typical Middle-Eastern flair.

- *450 g/1 lb macaroni or spaghetti*
- *Salt and freshly ground pepper*
- *50 g/2 oz finely chopped parsley*
- *5 or 6 finely chopped fresh mint or basil leaves*
- *90 ml/3 fl oz olive oil*
- *Juice of 1 lemon*

Bring a large saucepan of salted water to the boil, then add the pasta and a drop or two of oil. Bring back to the boil and simmer for about 15 minutes, or until just tender. Drain the pasta thoroughly before returning it to the pan.

Add the finely chopped herbs and toss with the pasta. Add the olive oil, lemon juice and salt and pepper to taste, and continue to toss until the pasta has absorbed most of the liquid. The dish may be served either hot or cold.

VEGETABLE LAYER

MOUSAKHA'A

SERVES 6

The name is the same as for the Greek dish of aubergines, mincemeat, potatoes and cheese, but the combination of vegetables and spices in this dish is utterly Middle Eastern. This is a main dish casserole, made complete with rice or burghul.

- *675 g/1½ lb aubergines or courgettes, washed, trimmed and cubed*
- *Salt and freshly ground pepper*
- *Olive oil*
- *2 large onions, sliced*
- *1 sweet green pepper, cored, seeded and chopped*
- *1 garlic clove, finely chopped*
- *675 g/1½ lb ripe tomatoes, peeled, seeded and chopped*
- *150 ml/¼ pint* Labneh *(page 53)*
- *2–3 eggs, beaten (optional)*

Put the aubergine cubes in a colander and sprinkle with salt. Allow them to drain for 30 minutes, then pat dry. (This process draws bitter juices out of the aubergines. If using courgettes, it is not necessary to salt and drain them.)

Pour about 30 ml/2 tbsp olive oil into a frying pan, and sauté the onions over medium heat for about 5 minutes, or until limp. Stir in the green pepper and cook for a further 3–4 minutes, until it is softened and the onions are lightly coloured. Stir in the garlic and remove from the heat. Use a slotted spoon to transfer the onions, pepper and garlic to a plate.

Heat more oil – about 45–60 ml/3–4 tbsp – and stir in the cubed aubergines or courgettes. Cook, stirring, for about 8 minutes, until they are coloured and beginning to soften. Pour off the excess oil and spread the aubergines or courgettes over the bottom of the pan. Place the onions and pepper evenly on top. Pour over the chopped tomatoes, and pat them even. Add about 250 ml/8 fl oz water to the pan, cover and simmer over low heat for 30 minutes. In the last 10 minutes of cooking time, top with spoonfuls of the *labneh* and the beaten egg, if desired. Cover and simmer until the eggs are set. Season the dish to taste and then serve.

LENTILS AND RICE
MUDARDARA

SERVES 6–8

Biblical anthropologists believe that Esau's "mess of pottage", as recorded in the Book of Genesis, was composed of rice and lentils – a version of the *mudardara* eaten today. Every family has its special way of making this staple, varying the proportions and/or the spicing. Cinnamon is not traditional, but it is sometimes added, since it is believed to increase sexual prowess and give strength to the ill.

- *175 g/6 oz brown lentils, washed and picked over*
- *75 ml/5 tbsp olive oil*
- *4 large onions, sliced*
- *225 g/8 oz long-grain rice, washed*
- *Salt and freshly ground pepper*
- *1.5 ml/¼ tsp cinnamon (optional)*

Bring a large saucepan of water to the boil, add the lentils, cover and simmer for about 25–30 minutes, until just soft.

Meanwhile, heat the olive oil in a flameproof casserole with a lid, and stir in the sliced onions. Cook over medium-low heat until the onions are limp and just beginning to colour. Remove half of them with a slotted spoon and set aside. Cook the remainder, being careful not to let them burn, until brown and glazed. Remove from the heat and transfer the onions to a bowl.

Drain the cooked lentils thoroughly, reserving the cooking liquid. Return the lightly cooked onions to the casserole and stir in the rice. Cook until the rice is just transparent, then stir in the drained lentils, salt and pepper to taste, the cinnamon, if desired, and enough of the cooking liquid to cover well. Cook the "pottage", covered, over low heat until the rice has absorbed all the water. If the rice and lentils are not tender yet, add a little more of the lentil liquid and cook until done. Stir in the caramelized onions and serve immediately.

LENTILS AND BURGHUL
IMJADRA

SERVES 6

This is a Lebanese alternative to *Mudardara* (this page) and, like that dish, serves as a staple of the poor. It is seen less in Beirut and the towns than in the countryside, where burghul still reigns supreme. It makes a substantial dish with a poached or fried egg on top of each serving. (Cooked chickpeas can be substituted for the cooked lentils.)

- *75 ml/5 tbsp olive oil*
- *3 onions, thinly sliced*
- *175 g/6 oz brown lentils, washed and picked over*
- *175 g/6 oz medium-ground burghul*
- *Salt and freshly ground pepper*
- *Cayenne pepper*

Heat the oil in a frying pan. Fry the onions until they are limp and lightly coloured – about 8–10 minutes. Remove about a third of the onions with a slotted spoon and reserve; continue to cook the remaining onions until they are browned. Reserve them.

In a flameproof casserole, cook the lentils in water to cover for about 25 minutes or until just tender. (Add more water during cooking, if necessary, but dot not make it too soupy.) Add the burghul, the light-coloured onions, salt, pepper and cayenne to taste. Stir to combine, cover, and let the burghul soak up the remaining moisture (add a bit more, if necessary) for about 10–12 minutes. Stir in the browned onions and serve immediately.

RICE WITH PINE NUTS AND CURRANTS

PILAU RICE

SERVES 4

Pilau rice has infiltrated Lebanon from the east – India and Iran – and from Turkey, to the north. It can contain influences from any of these cultures: pine nuts or pistachios, tamarind juice or saffron, currants or sultanas. This is a fairly simple version, which is often served moulded to accompany roasted fowl or other main courses.

- *90 ml/3 fl oz olive oil*
- *2 small onions, finely chopped*
- *60 ml/4 tbsp pine nuts*
- *30 ml/2 tbsp currants*
- *2.5 ml/½ tsp saffron threads*
- *450 g/1 lb long-grain rice*
- *Salt and freshly ground pepper*
- *Fresh parsley and coriander*
- *Ground paprika*

Heat the olive oil over medium heat and sauté the chopped onions until they are limp – about 6–8 minutes. Add the pine nuts and sauté for a few minutes more, until both the onions and nuts are lightly coloured. Stir in the currants, saffron and rice, and cook for about 1 minute or until the rice is just transparent.

Add salt to taste and pour in water to cover, about 750 ml/1¼ pints. Cook, covered, on high heat until the water begins to be absorbed, then turn the heat off and allow it to sit for about 20 minutes, or until all the water is absorbed and the rice tender. If it is still not tender, add a tablespoon or so more water and simmer for a couple of minutes. Then leave to sit for a further 5 minutes.

If desired, press the cooked rice into a mould(s) before turning out onto a plate garnished with parsley and coriander. Dust the rice with paprika.

POTATOES WITH CHICKPEAS
BATATAS BI HOUMUS

SERVES 6

This is another popular, filling dish, which can also do service as a main course. If served as a vegetarian main course, 450 g/1 lb fresh spinach can be stirred into the potatoes and chickpeas in the last 5 minutes of cooking and left to wilt.

- *120 ml/4 fl olive oil*
- *1 large onion, chopped*
- *350 ml/12 oz small red potatoes, washed and cut into small pieces*
- *2 garlic cloves, finely chopped*
- *225 g/8 oz cooked and drained chickpeas*
- *5 medium tomatoes, peeled, seeded and chopped Cayenne*
- *Cayene pepper*
- *2.5 ml/½ tsp coriander seeds*
- *Salt and freshly ground pepper*
- *50 g/2 oz finely chopped fresh parsley*

Heat the olive oil in a flameproof casserole with a cover. Add the onion and cook until it is lightly coloured and limp. Add the chopped potatoes and the garlic, and cook, stirring, over low heat for 3–4 minutes. Stir in the chickpeas, the tomatoes, cayenne pepper to taste and the coriander seeds.

Cover and simmer for 20 minutes, or until the potatoes are soft. Season to taste and stir in the chopped parsley before serving.

This dish can also be cooled, chilled overnight and served cold.

FRIED POTATOES
BATATAS HARRAS

SERVES 4–6

These fried potatoes are one of the spiciest dishes from the Lebanese kitchen, where cooks otherwise treat fresh chillies with respect. They are unashamedly oily and garlicky as well, so they are not for the faint-hearted or dyspeptic!

- *120 ml/4 fl oz olive oil*
- *675 g/1½ lb potatoes, peeled and chopped into small pieces*
- *Salt and freshly ground pepper*
- *3 garlic cloves, crushed*
- *2 hot chillies, seeded and chopped*
- *50 g/2 oz finely chopped coriander*

Heat the olive oil and drop in the potatoes. Fry over medium-hot heat and season to taste. Continue cooking for about 20 minutes until the potatoes are soft. Add the garlic and chillies, and gently toss the potatoes over the heat. Sprinkle over the coriander and serve.

BROWN BEANS WITH HERBS
FUL MEDAMES

SERVES 4–6

These small brown broad beans are members of the fava family, of a specific type native to Egypt and the Levant. They are served with egg on top for breakfast, mashed into a purée with extra oil and lemon juice for *mezze*, or prepared as in this recipe, for a *mezze*, for a main course with meats, or for a side dish. There are restaurants in the Middle East – Egypt especially – that specialize in *ful* dishes.

- *350 g/12 oz* ful medames *(brown beans), washed, picked over and soaked for 24 hours in a cool place*
- *75 ml/5 tbsp olive oil*
- *Juice of 1 lemon*
- *3 garlic cloves, crushed*
- *Salt and freshly ground pepper*
- *5 ml/1 tsp cumin*
- *45 ml/3 tbsp finely chopped fresh coriander*
- *Extra olive oil and lemon wedges (optional)*

Drain and rinse the beans. Bring a large saucepan – with just less than twice the volume of water to beans – to the boil and add the beans. Cover, bring to the boil again, reduce the heat and simmer for about 2½ hours, or until the beans are tender. Skim the top of the cooking liquid at the beginning to remove any scum. By the end of cooking, the water should have reduced and thickened. If the beans are still too soupy, strain off some of the liquid.

Stir in the oil, lemon juice, garlic, salt and pepper to taste, cumin and fresh coriander. Transfer the beans to a serving bowl and offer hot, or allow to cool and serve cold, with extra olive oil and lemon wedges.

SWEET POTATO AND OKRA KEBABS

SERVES 6

This is a modern recipe, combining the traditional vegetables of the countryside – okra and onions – with the more recently introduced sweet potato. The method of cooking, however, is time-honoured.

- *24 small okra (ladies' fingers)*
- *3 medium-sized sweet potatoes, peeled and each cut into 8 pieces*
- *24 pickling onions*
- *120 ml/4 fl oz olive oil*
- *15 ml/1 tbsp honey*
- *Salt and freshly ground pepper*
- *2.5 ml/½ tsp ground cumin*

Trim off the stem end of the okra, being careful not to cut into the seed chambers.

Bring a large saucepan of water to the boil. Drop in the sweet potato pieces and cook for 5 minutes. Add the onions and cook for 4 minutes, then add the okra and continue to cook for a further 1 minute. Drain the vegetables and plunge them into cold water to stop the cooking. Leave for a few minutes, then drain again. Peel the onions.

Thread the vegetables alternately onto 6 large or 12 small skewers. In a bowl, whisk together the oil, honey, salt and pepper to taste and cumin.

Baste the kebabs with the mixture and place them on a hot to medium-hot grill over grey-ashed coals (or alternatively under a preheated grill). Cook for 8–10 minutes, or until all the vegetables are tender, turning once and basting with the dressing occasionally. Serve immediately.

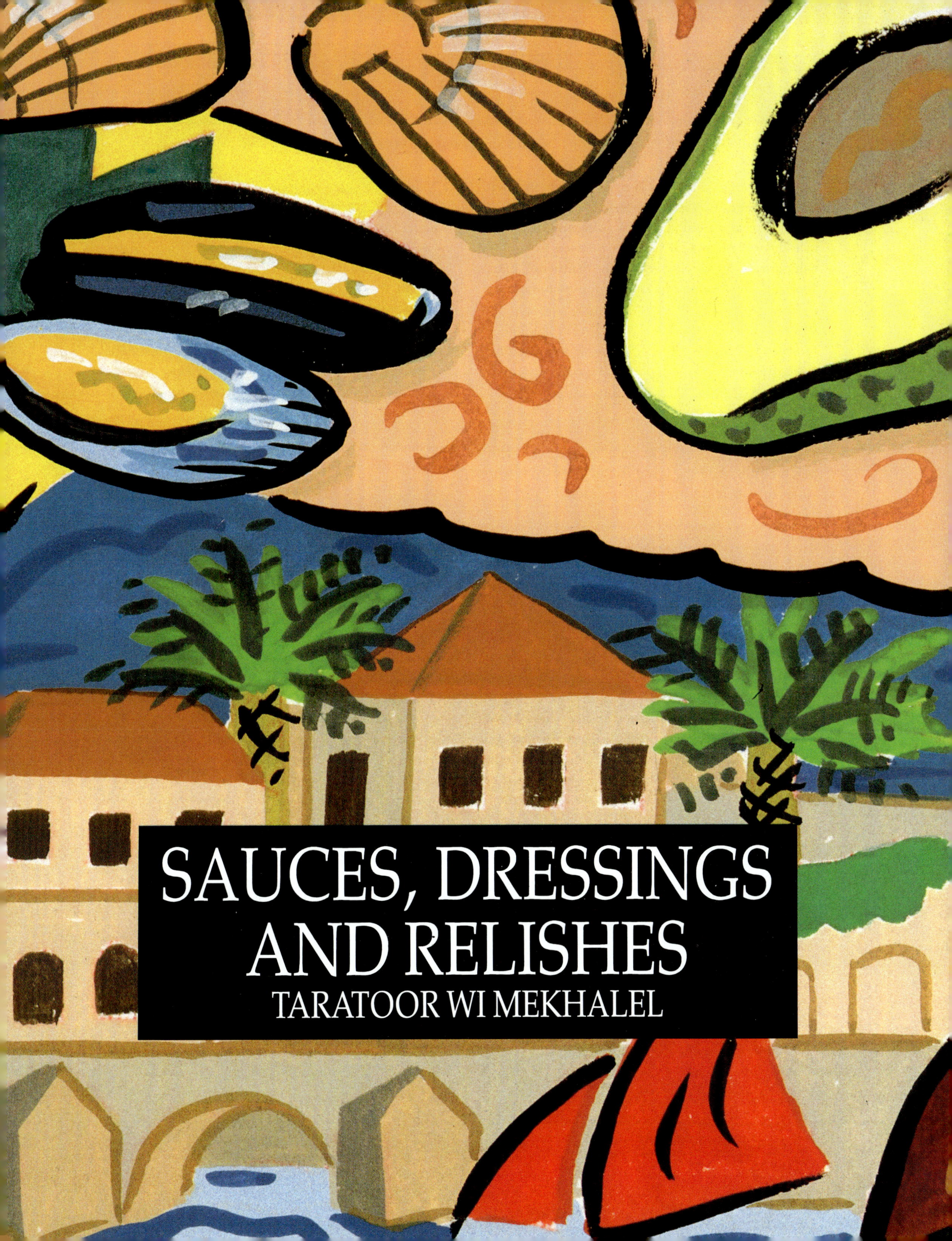

SAUCES, DRESSINGS AND RELISHES

TARATOOR WI MEKHALEL

PINE NUT SAUCE
TARATOOR BI SONOBA

MAKES ABOUT 450 ML/¾ PINT

This is another sauce that is usually partnered with fish, although to Western tastes it marries well with pasta, veal and poultry dishes. Although it is most usually served cold, it can also be used in cooking fish or meat. Try serving veal in the manner of *Vitello Tonnato*, substituting this *taratoor* for the tuna sauce.

- *1 garlic clove, crushed*
- *Salt*
- *2 slices white bread, crusts removed and cubed*
- *225 g/8 oz pine nuts*
- *1.5 ml/¼ tsp cayenne pepper*
- *Juice of 2 lemons*

Mash the garlic as much as possible in a bowl with a pinch of salt. Add the bread cubes, cover with warm water to soak and leave for 10 minutes.

Meanwhile place the pine nuts in the grinder of a blender, or in the bowl of a food processor fitted with a metal blade. When the nuts are finely chopped (if using the grinder, transfer the nuts to a liquidizing bowl), add the soaked bread, squeezed to remove some of the moisture, the garlic and the cayenne. Process a short time, then add the lemon juice, a little at a time, with the motor running. The result should be a rich, creamy sauce. If necessary, add a little more water. Serve immediately or cover and chill.

The sauce can be kept refrigerated for about 2 weeks or frozen.

PISTACHIO SAUCE
TARATOOR BI FOSTO

MAKES ABOUT 250 ML/8 FL OZ

Like other nut sauces this is cold, but it may be served with hot entrées – over fish or tossed with pasta – or cold, again with fish, veal or chicken. It is very rich, so use it sparingly. In Lebanon and other Arab countries, a very salty, aged cheese called *mesh* would be used, but aged *pecorino* makes an agreeable substitute.

- *150 g/5 oz shelled and toasted pistachios*
- *1 garlic clove, crushed*
- *30 ml/2 tbsp chopped parsley*
- *30 ml/2 tbsp fresh lemon juice*
- *45 ml/3 tbsp olive oil*
- *90 ml/3 fl oz Greek-style yoghurt*
- *25 g/1 oz grated aged* pecorino *cheese*

In the bowl of a blender or food processor fitted with a steel blade, put the pistachios, garlic and parsley. Run the motor for a brief time to roughly chop the mixture. Add the lemon juice and process until the mixture becomes smoother. With the motor running, slowly add the olive oil, 15 ml/1 tbsp at a time, until the sauce is emulsified. Finally, add the yoghurt and cheese, and process until smooth. Transfer the sauce to a bowl and serve immediately or chill.

The sauce may be refrigerated for up to 1 week. It does not freeze well.

COLD ALMOND SAUCE
NOUGADA

MAKES ABOUT 900 ML/1½ PINTS

This sweet and garlicky nut sauce is a close relative of *nougat*, a sweet brought home to Italy, Spain and France by the Crusaders. It is commonly served with cold white fish, chicken and turkey.

- *275 g/10 oz ground almonds*
- *Salt and freshly ground pepper*
- *1.5 ml/¼ tsp caster sugar*
- *2 garlic cloves, crushed*
- *Juice of 2 lemons*
- *120 ml/4 fl oz olive oil*
- *45 ml/3 tbsp finely chopped parsley*

In a bowl, combine the ground almonds with salt and pepper to taste and the sugar. Mix well. Mash the garlic into the dry ingredients until it has been ground into the almonds. Slowly stir in the lemon juice and then beat in the olive oil, a little at a time, until the sauce is thick as desired. (This can also be done in a food processor or blender, but the result will lack texture.)

When the sauce is emulsified, stir in the chopped parsley. Serve immediately or cover and chill.

The sauce can be kept refrigerated for 2 weeks, and it can also be frozen.

SESAME SAUCE
TARATOOR BI TAHINI

MAKES ABOUT 450 ML/¾ PINT

This is the most frequently encountered of Lebanese sauces. It is served heated or cold with both fish and vegetables. It bears a superficial resemblance to Indonesian peanut sauce *(gado-gado)* in its almost overpowering nuttiness.

- *2 garlic cloves, crushed*
- *4 ml/¾ tsp salt*
- *Large pinch of cayenne*
- *250 ml/8 fl oz* tahini *paste*
- *150 ml/¼ pint lemon juice*

In a bowl, mash the garlic together with the salt and cayenne until it makes a paste. Whisk in the *tahini* with a fork, then thin the mixture with the juice, beating continuously. Serve the sauce immediately or cover and chill.

The sauce can be kept refrigerated for 2 weeks, and it can also be frozen.

CLASSIC VINAIGRETTE

MAKES ABOUT 250 ML/8 FL OZ

This can be made into a "classic" vinaigrette, in the French-Lebanese sense, by using the Dijon mustard and the wine vinegar (or a combination of vinegar and juice), or in the Arabic-Lebanese tradition, by omitting the mustard and using only lemon juice.

- *2.5 ml/½ tsp Dijon mustard (optional)*
- *45 ml/3 tbsp red wine vinegar or lemon juice, or a combination of the two*
- *120 ml/4 fl oz olive oil*
- *Salt and freshly ground pepper*

Combine the mustard, if used, the vinegar/lemon juice and the oil in a bottle with a screw top. Shake hard until the dressing is emulsified. Add salt and pepper to taste and shake again. Use immediately, or keep in a dark, cool place for up to 2 weeks.

MIXED PICKLES

KABBIS

MAKES 450 G/1 LB

Pickles can be mixed together before pickling; as with our Western piccalilli, the best combination is probably cauliflower, small onions, cucumbers and, perhaps, green beans. Otherwise, if you are using vegetables such as small green plum tomatoes or turnips, which do not look appetizing pickled, the pickles are traditionally dyed by adding beetroot juice.

- *450 g/1 lb mixed or selected vegetables: turnips, aubergines, small onions, cauliflower, cucumber, green plum tomatoes, green beans*
- *450 ml/16 fl oz white wine vinegar*
- *250 ml/8 fl oz water (if desired, use water in which beetroot has been cooked)*
- *30 ml/2 tbsp salt*

Use only very small turnips, aubergines, cucumbers, onions and tomatoes. Blanch the vegetables first, drain thoroughly, then cut them as appropriate.

The turnips, aubergines and cucumbers should be quartered, the tomatoes halved and the onions used whole. The green beans should be cut into 5 cm/2 in lengths and the cauliflower cut into florets.

Divide the vegetables between pickling jars or plastic-capped screw-top jars. (Do not use metal-capped jars.) In a pitcher, mix together the vinegar, water (coloured or not) and salt. Fill the jars almost to the brim with the vegetables, then pour in the pickling liquid to cover just below the screw top. Tap the jars a couple of times on a hard surface to settle the vegetables and expel the air. Cover each jar with stretched plastic film and then with the screw top.

Store the pickles in a cool, dark place for up to 3 months. They are best if left for at least 1 month.

CUMIN-LEMON DRESSING

MAKES ABOUT 250 ML/8 FL OZ

This spicy vinaigrette makes an interesting change from the more classic versions. It complements a simple tomato salad, pulses such as cold cooked lentils, or even leftovers – such as cold roast potatoes, cubed and tossed with red onion rings and chopped flat-leaved parsley. That is the way the Lebanese and Syrians use it.

- *15 ml/1 tbsp caster sugar*
- *7.5 ml/1½ tsp ground cumin*
- *Large pinch of turmeric*
- *75 ml/5 tbsp fresh lemon juice*
- *120 ml/4 fl oz olive oil*

Combine the sugar, cumin, tumeric and lemon juice in a bottle with a screw top. Shake hard to dissolve the sugar, then add the olive oil and shake again until the dressing is emulsified. Use immediately, or store in a cool, dark place for up to 2 weeks.

YOGHURT AND CUCUMBER SAUCE

MAKES ABOUT 475 ML/16 FL OZ

This is an extremely simple sauce, a relative of the Turkish salad *Caçik* (page 59), which is often served as an accompaniment to *Shwarma* (page 13) or over meat-stuffed vegetables, such as aubergines and courgettes. Mint or coriander, as desired, lends a distinctive flavour.

- *1 garlic clove, crushed*
- *Salt and freshly ground pepper to taste*
- *250 ml/8 fl oz Greek-style yoghurt*
- *1 small or 1½ large cucumber, peeled, seeded and grated*
- *30 ml/w tbsp finely chopped fresh mint or coriander*

In a bowl, mash the garlic and about 5 ml/1 tsp salt together. Stir in the yoghurt, cucumber and the mint or coriander. Taste, season further to taste, stir again, and serve immediately or chill.

This sauce can be refrigerated for up to 1 week. It does not freeze well.

PISTACHIO DRESSING

MAKES ABOUT 250 ML/8 FL OZ

This is a light salad dressing suited to mixed green salads (see Mixed Bitter Leaf Salad, page 44) or sliced avocados.

- *60 ml/4 tbsp fresh lemon juice*
- *120 ml/4 fl oz olive oil*
- *5 ml/1 tsp grated lemon peel*
- *4 spring onions, finely chopped*
- *50 g/2 oz crushed salted, shelled pistachios*
- *Salt and freshly ground pepper*

In a bowl, whisk the olive oil into the lemon juice. Add the lemon peel, onion, crushed nuts and season to taste. Whisk again to combine thoroughly, then use immediately or bottle.

The dressing will keep in a cool, dark place for as long as 3 days.

GREEN MAYONNAISE

MAKES ABOUT 450 ML/16 FL OZ

Mayonnaise is not indigenous to Lebanese cuisine; yoghurt or *tahini* traditionally does service when a creamy cold sauce/dressing is called for. However, the demands and preferences of a multitude of Western visitors – particularly the French – imposed their influence, and mayonnaise has become commonplace at large hotels and Continental-style restaurants. It often comes from a bottle, however, "improved" with herbs to impart an interesting Middle-Eastern tang.

- *350 ml/12 fl oz homemade or good commercial mayonnaise*
- *75 g/3 oz finely chopped coriander*
- *75 g/3 oz finely chopped flat-leaved parsley*
- *60 ml/4 tbsp finely chopped fresh dill*
- *Large pinch cayenne*
- *30 ml/2 tbsp fresh lemon juice*

Combine all the ingredients in a blender or food processor fitted with a metal blade. Process until the mayonnaise is smooth and thickly green-flecked.

Use immediately or chill for up to 3 days.

LEMON RELISH

MAKES ABOUT 450 ML/16 FL OZ

This zesty chutney has its roots in North African cuisine, where whole pickled lemons are frequently used in cooking. It has been adapted to serve as a sophisticated accompaniment to fish or fowl by French-trained Lebanese cooks, who have substituted white wine for the brine more commonly encountered in North African countries.

- *10 large lemons*
- *30 ml/2 tbsp sunflower oil*
- *2 small onions, finely chopped*
- *250 ml/8 fl oz dry white wine*
- *175 g/6 oz caster sugar*
- *2.5 ml/½ tsp cayenne pepper*
- *2.5 ml/½ tsp cumin seeds*
- *7.5 ml/1½ tsp freshly ground black pepper*

Using a vegetable peeler, remove the rind from all 10 lemons in large strips, including as little pith as possible. Chop the peel finely and reserve.

Take 2 of the peeled lemons, cut the flesh away from the pith and roughly chop the fruit. Pick out the seeds and discard them.

In a heavy saucepan, heat the oil and add the chopped onion. Sauté carefully for about 10 minutes until it is limp, but not coloured. Stir in the peel, chopped lemon flesh, white wine, sugar and spices. Cook over a medium-high heat for about 20 minutes, until the liquid has almost disappeared and the relish is syrupy.

Transfer the relish to a bowl to cool, then chill. Serve immediately or keep chilled and well covered for up to 2 weeks.

GARLIC SAUCE
TARATOOR BI SADE

MAKES ABOUT 250 ML/8 FL OZ

Although this is called a sauce and is used as such, particularly with poultry and lamb dishes, it is also useful as a garlic-flavoured base for a wide variety of other dishes. Thinned with yoghurt, it makes a delicious, if powerful, dip. It is glorious when used to replace some of the milk in mashed potatoes, and completely changes classic ratatouille. Use your imagination – and courage!

- *45 garlic cloves, skinned and crushed*
- *150 ml/¼ pint olive oil*
- *Juice of 1 lemon*

Traditionally, this is made by hand, pounding the garlic with a mortar and pestle and then beating in the olive oil and lemon juice. Today it is more easily made in a food processor fitted with a metal blade, or in a blender.

Put the garlic into the processor bowl and blend briefly to chop the garlic finely. Then slowly add the oil in a stream with the motor running. You should have a smooth purée. Finally, add the lemon juice. Blend briefly and transfer to a bowl. Serve immediately.

The sauce can be kept refrigerated for 2 weeks or more, or frozen.

SATSUMA DRESSING

MAKES ABOUT 250 ML/8 FL OZ

This sweet-tangy dressing goes marvellously well with tart fruit salads (like Grapefruit and Avocado Compote, page 62) or over chicken, turkey – or, in a non-Lebanese mode – ham salad.

- *30 ml/2 tbsp honey*
- *5 ml/1 tsp finely grated satsuma peel*
- *120 ml/4 fl oz freshly squeezed satsuma juice*
- *30 ml/2 tbsp freshly squeezed lemon juice*
- *45 ml/3 tbsp sunflower oil*

Place the honey and satsuma peel in a bowl, and carefully beat in the satsuma juice and lemon juice. When fully combined, beat in the oil. Use the dressing immediately or bottle it.

The dressing will keep up to 2 weeks when stored in a cool, dark place.

BREADS AND DESSERTS

KHOUBZ WI HAELAWIYAT

LEBANESE BREAD
KHOUBZ

MAKES 8 ROUNDS

Versions of this bread are found all over the Arab world, made at village bakeries and in backyard ovens of packed earth. The recipe is a simple one, but the bread itself is heavenly – a light, puffy round with a slightly gritty quality. It must be eaten immediately, however, as it becomes hard and crumbly as it stands, unless it is quickly covered.

- *40 g/1½ oz fresh or 2 packets (12 g/1½ oz) dry yeast*
- *900 g/2 lb chapati flour or strong white bread flour*
- *7.5 ml/1½ tsp salt*
- *60 ml/2 fl oz olive oil*
- *Chapati flour or cornmeal*

In a bowl combine 60 ml/2 fl oz lukewarm water with the fresh yeast. Let it stand for about 3 minutes, then stir to make sure that all of the yeast is dissolved. Allow to rest in a warm place for 6 minutes, or until it has doubled in size.

Put the flour in a large, warmed bowl and stir in the salt. Make a well in the centre and pour in the yeast mixture. Add the oil and 475 ml/16 fl oz lukewarm water, working the latter in a few tablespoons at a time. Add a little more, if necessary, to make a firm dough that can be picked up and removed to a floured work surface.

Knead the dough, pressing, pushing and folding it, for about 20 minutes, or until it is smooth and elastic. Transfer the dough to the bowl, cover with a tea towel and leave in a warm place for 2 hours, until doubled in bulk and bubbly. Place the dough on the work surface and "knock it back" with a couple of knuckle punches. Divide the dough into 8 pieces and shape them into balls.

Scatter the chapati flour or cornmeal on the work surface, and roll out 4 of the balls into 20 cm/8 in rounds. As you roll out each round, place it on a baking tray covered with a tea towel. Repeat with the remaining 4 balls on another baking tray. Leave both covered trays of bread to rise for another half hour. Preheat the oven to 200°C/400°F/Gas Mark 6.

Place both trays, one above the other, as low in the oven as possible. Bake at this level for 5 minutes, then move them to the centre of the oven, placing the tray that was lower on top. Continue baking for a further 4–5 minutes, or until the rounds are puffed and golden. Remove from the oven and serve immediately. The rounds can be kept covered in aluminium foil in a low oven or warm place, if not needed immediately, but they will loose their puffy quality quickly.

SESAME BREAD RINGS

KA'AK

MAKES 12

In Lebanon these sesame rings are made by bakeries; in some other countries they are more commonly sold on street corners. The *mahlab* (page 15) imparts a typical flavour found only in Arab baked goods. Broken into pieces, *ka'ak* makes a good alternative to pitta or *khoubz* for dips.

- *8 g/⅓ oz fresh or 1 packet (6 g/¼ oz) dry yeast*
- *5 ml/1 tsp caster sugar*
- *225 g/8 oz strong white bread flour*
- *2.5 ml/½ tsp salt*
- *5 ml/1 tsp ground* mahlab
- *15 ml/1 tbsp* semnah *or melted butter*
- *1 egg, beaten*
- *45 g/3 tbsp sesame seeds*

In a bowl combine 60 ml/2 fl oz lukewarm water with the yeast and caster sugar. Let it stand for about 3 minutes, then stir. Allow to rest in a warm place for about 6 minutes.

Put the flour in a large, warmed bowl, and stir in the salt and ground *mahlab*. Make a well in the centre and pour in the yeast and sugar mixture. Work the *semnah* or butter into the flour and add 75–120 ml/5–6½ tbsp water to the dough, a spoonful at a time, until you have a firm dough that can be moved to a floured work surface.

Preheat the oven to 150°C/300°F/Gas Mark 2.

Knead the dough, pressing, pushing and folding, for about 10 minutes, until it is smooth and elastic. Transfer to a bowl, cover with a tea towel and leave in a warm place for 15 minutes.

"Knock back" the dough with a couple of punches and divide it into 12 pieces. On a floured work surface, roll each piece into a long "sausage" about the thickness of a finger. Shape the sausage into a circle – or, less authentically but more decoratively, into a criss-crossed pretzel shape.

Place the rings on an oiled baking tray, cover with a tea towel and leave to rise for about 15 minutes. Brush each ring with some beaten egg and sprinkle with sesame seeds. Bake in the oven for about 30–35 minutes, until golden.

Transfer the rings to a cake rack to cool for 10 minutes before serving. The rings freeze successfully.

PINE NUT MACAROONS

MAKES ABOUT 35 MACAROONS

These biscuits are a contribution of the once-large Italian community in Beirut; they combine the flavours of Rome and the Middle East to great effect.

- *225 g/8 oz marzipan*
- *100 g/4 oz caster sugar*
- *1.5 ml/¼ tsp vanilla or lemon essence*
- *Pinch of cinnamon*
- *Pinch of allspice*
- *2 egg whites*
- *60 ml/4 tbsp pine nuts*
- *Icing sugar*

In a large bowl, using an electric mixer, beat together the marzipan and caster sugar until creamy; beat in the vanilla or lemon essence and the spices. One at at time, beat in the egg whites.

Preheat the oven to 150°C/300°F/Gas Mark 2.

When the mixture is smooth, drop the batter by small spoonfuls onto baking tray(s) covered with greaseproof paper, leaving space between each mound, and stick the pine nuts into the macaroons so that they look like porcupine quills.

Bake the macaroons for about 15 minutes, until the biscuits and nuts are light gold. Remove the tray(s) from the oven, lift the edges of the greaseproof paper, and pour a thin stream of water under the paper to loosen the macaroons. Lift them with a spatula to wire racks and let them cool completely before serving.

The macaroons will keep in an airtight container for as much as 1 week.

ARMENIAN FLATBREAD

MAKES 2 ROUND LOAVES

The sizeable Armenian community in Lebanon – established there as a result of several Turkish massacres – have made several contributions to the national cuisine. This flatbread makes an interesting change to *khoubz* when bread is called for. Each loaf will serve about 4–6.

- *18 g/¾ oz fresh or 1 packet (6 g/¼ oz) dry yeast*
- *5 ml/1 tsp caster sugar*
- *350 g/12 oz strong bread flour*
- *5 ml/1 tsp salt*
- *5 ml/1 tsp* semnah *or soft butter*
- *30 ml/2 tbsp yoghurt*
- *30–45 ml/2–3 tbsp poppy seeds*

In a bowl, combine 250 ml/8 fl oz lukewarm water with the yeast. Let it stand for about 3 minutes, then stir in the sugar and allow to stand in a warm place for about 10–12 minutes, or until it is bubbly and doubled in size.

Put half of the flour into a large, warmed bowl and stir in the salt. Make a well in the centre and work in the *semnah,* then add the yeast mixture, little by little, until you have a workable dough.

Remove the dough to a floured work surface and knead it, pressing, pushing and folding it, for about 10 minutes, adding as much of the remaining flour as is necessary to make it smooth and elastic. Transfer it back to the bowl, cover with a tea towel and leave to rise in a warm place for about 45 minutes, or until it is doubled in size.

Preheat the oven to 200°C/400°F/Gas Mark 6. Knock back the dough with a couple of knuckle punches, and divide it in half. Shape it into 2 balls, then roll out each ball into a 40 cm/15 in-diameter circle. Brush the two loaves with the yoghurt, thinned with a little water, and sprinkle over the poppy seeds. Bake for 20–25 minutes until the bread becomes golden brown and puffed.

You can freeze one or both loaves, if desired, to be warmed up at a later date.

YOGHURT WITH HONEY AND NUTS

SERVES 4

This dish can be made very simply, using yoghurt straight from the carton. However, it benefits from letting the yoghurt drain for a little while to thicken it – though not as long as for *labneh*.

- *750 ml/1¼ pints Greek-style sheep's yoghurt*
- *50 g/2 oz whole blanched almonds, roughly chopped*
- *50 g/2 oz whole pistachios, halved*
- *30 ml/2 tbsp honey*
- *5 ml/1 tsp ground cinnamon*
- *5 ml/1 tsp ground nutmeg or cardamom*

Pour the yoghurt into a colander lined with damp muslin or a clean, fine-weave dishcloth. Let it drain in this position for about 2–3 hours.

Preheat the oven to 180°C/350°F/Gas Mark 4.

Mix the two nuts on a baking tray and toast until golden – about 8–10 minutes. Transfer the nuts into a bowl and stir in the honey and cinnamon.

Transfer the drained yoghurt into 4 small bowls and spoon over the honeyed nuts. Sprinkle each portion with a little of the nutmeg or cardamom, as preferred. Serve immediately.

SEMOLINA LEMON CAKE
BASBOOSA

MAKES A 20 X 30 CM/8 X 12 IN CAKE

This lemon-flavoured cake is popular from Turkey to Egypt, and is served either as a teatime treat or as a dessert. The traditional version is richer in *semnah* than this one, which cuts the fat content considerably.

- *225 g/8 oz caster sugar*
- *225 g/8 oz semolina*
- *2.5 ml/½ tsp bicarbonate of soda*
- *350 ml/12 fl oz Greek-style yoghurt*
- *60 ml/4 tbsp* semnah *or melted butter*
- *18–24 whole blanched almonds*

SYRUP

- *225 g/8 oz caster sugar*
- *60 ml/4 tbsp fresh lemon juice*
- *Few drops rosewater*

Make the syrup first. Put 350 ml/12 fl oz water, the sugar and the lemon juice into a heavy-based saucepan and simmer, stirring, until the sugar has dissolved. Then bring the mixture to a vigorous boil, and cook until it has the consistency of golden syrup or registers 108°C/220°F on a sugar thermometer. Put aside to cool.

Preheat the oven to 180°C/350°F/Gas Mark 4.

To make the cake, mix together the first 3 dry ingredients. Beat in the yoghurt with a wooden spoon, then beat in the *semnah* or melted butter. Scrape the batter into a well-greased 20 x 30 cm/8 x 12 in baking tin, and bake for about 15 minutes. Top the cake with the blanched almonds, spacing them 3 or 4 nuts across and 6 down. Continue to bake the cake for a further 30 minutes or until golden.

Cool the cake for about 10 minutes, then cut it into squares or diamonds. Pour the cooled syrup over the cake slowly, allowing it to soak in; use only enough to saturate the cake; it should not be soggy. Serve at room temperature.

The cake will keep in an airtight container for anything up to a week.

STUFFED DATES
TAMAR BI LOHZ

MAKES 12 OF EACH

Stuffed dried fruits – sweetmeats – are part of traditional Arab hospitality, offered to guests to while away the time while talking and/or drinking coffee or tea. The old recipes for some fillings are very sweet – simply pastes of sugar and ground almonds or flower waters. This version, which can be adapted to dried prunes, substituting walnuts for the almonds, is more appealing to modern tastes.

- *12 plump medjul dates*
- *100 g/4 oz* anari *or ricotta cheese*
- *5 ml/1 tsp caster sugar*
- *5 ml/1 tsp finely grated fresh lemon rind*
- *12 whole almonds*

Carefully slit the dates and remove the pits; gently open up the hole created. Set aside.

In a bowl combine thoroughly the cheese, sugar and lemon rind. Divide the mixture between the 12 dates, pushing it into the cavities and moulding the dates around the filling. Push an almond into the top of each date. Arrange attractively on a small serving plate.

HONEY CAKES

MAKES ABOUT 40

These biscuit-like cakes combine three favourite Middle-Eastern flavours: honey, cinnamon and lemon. The recipe is a variation of a Jewish favourite; in the 1970s the Jewish community was still a small but influential part of Beirut.

- *450 ml/16 fl oz* semnah *or olive oil*
- *225 g/8 oz light brown sugar*
- *15 ml/1 tbsp ground cloves*
- *15 ml/1 tbsp ground cinnamon*
- *5 ml/1 tsp grated lemon rind*
- *Juice of 2 lemons*
- *120 ml/4 fl oz honey*
- *½ cup/120 ml/4 fl oz milk*
- *575 g/1¼ lb plain flour*
- *30 ml/2 tbsp baking powder*

GLAZE

- *450 ml/16 fl oz water*
- *250 ml/8 fl oz honey*
- *250 g/8 oz caster sugar*
- *5 ml/1 tsp fresh lemon juice*
- *100 g/4 oz mixed peel*

In a bowl, beat together the *semnah* or oil and the sugar with an electric mixer until creamy. Add the cloves, cinnamon, lemon rind and juice, and continue beating for about 5 minutes until thoroughly combined. Beat in the honey and milk. On low speed, add the flour and baking powder a little at a time. Continue to mix slowly for between 10 and 15 minutes until you have a smooth dough.

Preheat the oven to 180°C/350°F/Gas Mark 4.

Pick out pieces of dough and roll into plum-sized balls. Flatten the balls between the hands and make a slight indentation across the centre. Place on greased baking trays. Bake for about 20 minutes, or until they are lightly golden.

Just before the cakes are done, heat the water and stir in the honey and caster sugar. Bring the mixture to a boil; stir until the sugar is dissolved. Lower the heat and simmer for about 5 minutes; the syrup should thicken slightly. Take the mixture off the heat and stir in the lemon juice.

When the cakes are done, remove one at a time from the baking trays with a spatula and dip into the syrup to coat thoroughly. Place the cakes on a rack, sprinkle with the mixed peel, and let the cakes become sticky-dry. They will keep in an airtight tin, but separate the layers with greaseproof paper.

Stuffed Dates.

CINNAMON-PISTACHIO CRESCENTS

MAKES ABOUT 48 CRESCENTS

The crescent or half-moon shape has always been a popular one in Arab lore. These sweet pastries bear some resemblance to miniature French croissants, but with a distinctly Levantine flavour.

- *18 g/¾ oz fresh or 1 packet (6 g/¼ oz) dry yeast*
- *30 ml/2 tbsp caster sugar*
- *275 g/10 oz plain flour*
- *250 ml/8 fl oz melted butter*
- *2 eggs, beaten*

FILLING

- *15 ml/1 tbsp ground cinnamon*
- *100 g/4 oz light brown sugar*
- *50 g/2 oz finely crushed pistachios*

In a bowl, combine 60 ml/2 fl oz lukewarm water with the yeast. Leave it to rest for 3 minutes, then stir in the sugar and leave for about 5 minutes to allow the sugar to dissolve.

Put the flour in a large bowl, make a well and stir in the yeast mixture, the melted butter and the beaten eggs. Mix with the hands until well combined. Form into a ball, cover the bowl with plastic film and chill for at least 4 hours or overnight.

Preheat the oven to 180°C/350°F/Gas Mark 4.

In a bowl, mix together the cinnamon, brown sugar and nuts. Transfer the ball of dough to a floured work surface and divide it into 6 equal balls.

Roll out one ball into a 20 cm/8 in round. Spoon out one-sixth of the cinnamon-nut mixture onto a plate. Press the dough round into the mixture, cover with another plate, and turn the circle backwards onto the second plate. Shake any cinnamon mixture remaining on the plate onto the round. Divide the dough circle into 8 wedges and roll each wedge up, beginning at the wide end. Curve the ends in a half-moon shape. Let the crescents rest for 20 minutes before putting them in the oven for baking.

Repeat the process with the remaining dough balls and cinnamon-nut mixture. Bake the crescents in batches on oiled baking trays for 15 minutes, or until they are golden.

Some or all of the crescents can be frozen to be warmed up at a later time.

PHYLLO AND NUT PASTRIES

BAKLAVA

MAKES A 20 X 39 CM/8 X 12 IN CAKE

This recipe has variants all over the Middle East. Although we are perhaps more familiar with the Greek or Turkish version, containing walnuts and using honey in the syrup, the Lebanese use pistachios and/or cashews, and substitute orange blossom water for honey. When shaped into small "cigars", they are called *Asabieh*.

- *450 g/1 lb commercial phyllo pastry sheets*
- *225 g/8 oz* semnah *or unsalted butter, melted*
- *60 ml/4 tbsp sunflower oil*
- *400 g/14 oz shelled pistachios or cashews, finely chopped*
- *15 ml1 tbsp caster sugar*
- *2.5 ml/½ tsp ground cinnamon*

SYRUP

- *350 g/12 oz caster sugar*
- *15 ml/1 tbsp fresh lemon juice*
- *15 ml/1 tbsp orange blossom water*

Make the syrup. Combine the sugar, lemon juice and 175 ml/6 fl oz water in a heavy saucepan, and simmer over medium heat until the sugar dissolves. Bring the syrup to the boil and cook vigorously for 5 minutes, until it thickens and reaches 108°C/220°F on a sugar thermometer. Remove the pan from the heat, stir in the orange blossom water, let it cool, then chill it.

Preheat the oven to 180°C/350°F/Gas Mark 4.

Take the phyllo sheets out of the packet and cover with a damp cloth. Generously grease the bottom and sides of a 20 x 30 cm/8 x 12 in baking tin with some of the butter, then mix the remaining butter with the sunflower oil.

Unroll or unfold two sheets of the phyllo, and drape one into the baking tin, pressing it into the corners. Brush the sheet with some of the *semnah*/butter and oil, and place the other sheet on top. Brush that sheet with the fat as well, then fold down the two pieces of excess phyllo pastry into the baking tin, and brush with oil and butter. Repeat the process with 2 more sheets of pastry. Continue until half the phyllo sheets have been used.

In a bowl, mix together the chopped nuts, sugar and cinnamon. Scatter the mixture over the phyllo in the baking tin and pat it down evenly. Cover the nuts with two more sheets of phyllo pastry, brushed with the *semnah*/butter and oil and folded down. Finish with pairs of the remaining sheets of oiled phyllo, and brush the top with the remaining butter and oil mixture.

Score the top into 2-in/5-cm diamond-shaped servings. Bake the *baklava* for 45 minutes at 160°C/325°F/Gas Mark 3, then to 200°C/400°F/Gas Mark 6 for 20 minutes, until the top is crisp and golden brown.

Remove the *baklava* from the oven, pour over as much cooled syrup as the cake can absorb, and let it cool. Serve at room temperature or chilled.

STUFFED DOUGH PASTRIES

MAM'OUL

MAKES ABOUT 30 PASTRIES

These round or egg-shaped little *petits fours* have much the same consistency as Scandinavian or Dutch *spritz* biscuits. They can be seen lined up on the counters of Middle Eastern pâtisseries, dusted with bright green crushed pistachio.

- *175 g/6 oz unsalted butter*
- *350 g/12 oz plain flour*
- *15 ml/1 tbsp rosewater*
- *30 ml/2 tbsp milk*
- *Icing sugar*
- *30 ml/2 tbsp finely crushed or ground pistachio nuts*

DATE FILLING

- *175 g/6 oz chopped sugared dates*

NUT FILLING

- *100 g/4 oz pistachios or walnuts*
- *Caster sugar*

Make the date filling first. Pour 120 ml/4 fl oz water over the chopped dates, and stir over low heat until the dates and water have become an almost dry mush. Reserve.

Cut the butter into the flour and mix together with the fingers; add the rosewater and just enough milk to bind the dough. Continue to work until the dough is soft and pliable. Divide the dough into 30 small balls and then into two groups of 15 balls each.

Flatten a ball slightly and press the side of your index finger down the centre to form a hollow. Fill carefully with a little of the date mixture, and re-shape the dough to enclose it, making a round or an oval biscuit. Repeat this process of filling with the 14 remaining balls in the group.

Flatten and fill the remaining 15 balls in the same way, but using the crushed pistachios or walnuts and a pinch of sugar.

Preheat the oven to 160°C/325°F/Gas Mark 3.

Place the pastries on a baking tray and score lengthwise along the top with a small fork. Bake for about 20–25 minutes; they should not be allowed to brown. Remove from the oven and allow them to cool and harden, then roll in the icing sugar. Take a pinch of the finely crushed or ground pistachio nuts, and sprinkle it down the scored tops of the *mam'oul*.

The biscuits will keep in an airtight container for about 1 week.

CINNAMON ICE CREAM

MAKES ABOUT 750 ML/1¼ PINTS

Ice cream, unlike sorbet or sherbert, is not a traditional Arab or Lebanese sweet. However, as elsewhere throughout the modern world, it has become an accepted part of the culture. This cinnamon ice cream is redolent of the spice market. It goes equally well with fresh fruit salad or *Basboosa* (page 117).

- *600 ml/1 pint double cream*
- *2 egg whites*
- *10 ml/2 tsp ground cinnamon*
- *175 g/6 oz caster sugar*

Place the cream in a large bowl and stir 10 ml/2 tbsp cold water into it. Put the cream and the metal whisks from an electric mixer into the refrigerator, and chill for about 1 hour.

Remove the whisks and cream from the refrigerator and whisk the cream until it has trebled in volume. In another bowl, beat the egg whites until they hold stiff peaks. Gently fold the cinnamon and sugar into the cream, then follow with the beaten egg whites.

Pour the mixture into a plastic container and freeze for 4 hours. Remove from the container into the bowl of a food processor fitted with a metal blade, and process until the ice cream is smooth. Return to the container and freeze for at least 6 hours or overnight.

LEBANESE BREAD PUDDING
OSMALIYEH

SERVES 6

This Arabian dessert is variously made with phyllo pastry, bread or sweet biscuits, but this version is the most homely – as bread pudding should be.

- *Oil for frying*
- *6–7 individual rounds of* khoubz *(Arab bread) or pitta, split and torn into shreds*
- *100 g/4 oz plump raisins*
- *100 g/4 oz mixed almonds and pistachios*
- *75 g/3 oz chopped ready-to-eat dried apricots*
- *100 g/4 oz caster sugar*
- *1 l/1¾ pints milk*
- *300 ml/½ pint double cream*
- *7.5 ml/1½ tsp ground cinnamon*

Heat the oil until it is very hot and test with a shred of bread. If it turns a golden brown, then add more pieces and fry the bread in batches. Drain on absorbent paper.

Spread two-thirds of the fried bread across the bottom of a baking dish, overlapping the pieces. Sprinkle the raisins, nuts and apricots over it evenly. Cover with the remaining fried bread, roughly crushed.

Preheat the oven to 200°C/400°F/Gas Mark 6.

In a saucepan, stir together the milk, the cream and three-quarters of the sugar. Bring to the boil, then remove from the heat and pour over the bread and fruit mixture in the baking dish.

Mix together the remaining sugar and the cinnamon, and sprinkle over the top of the pudding. Bake for 20 minutes, until browned and bubbling. Serve immediately.

PISTACHIO-ORANGE CAKE

MAKES A 23 CM/9 IN SQUARE CAKE

This is another Lebanese syrup cake. The invention of a French-trained chef from Beirut, it reveals its European provenance in the use of ground nuts in the batter and liqueur in the syrup.

- *3 large eggs*
- *60 g/2½ oz caster sugar*
- *2.5 ml/½ tsp vanilla or lemon extract*
- *7.5 ml/1½ tsp finely grated orange rind*
- *Pinch of cinnamon*
- *Pinch of cream of tartar*
- *225 g/8 oz shelled pistachios, finely ground*
- *25 g/1 oz ground* ka'ak *or crisp bread crumbs*

SYRUP

- *100 g/4 oz caster sugar*
- *30 ml/2 tbsp fresh orange juice*
- *2–3 kumquats, thinly sliced*
- *30 ml/2 tbsp Cointreau or Grand Marnier*

Make the syrup first. In a heavy-based saucepan, combine the sugar, orange juice and sliced kumquats, and 250 ml/4 fl oz water. Simmer over moderate heat until the sugar is dissolved, then bring to the boil and cook until the syrup has thickened (and registers 110°C/220°F on a sugar thermometer). Take off the heat and stir in the orange liqueur. Leave to cool.

Preheat the oven to 180°C/350°F/Gas Mark 4.

To make the cake, separate the 3 eggs and beat the egg yolks with the sugar and vanilla in a bowl with an electric mixer until the mixture is light yellow. Stir in the grated rind and cinnamon. In another bowl, beat the egg whites with the cream of tartar until they hold soft peaks. In a third bowl, mix together the ground nuts and *ka'ak* crumbs. Fold one-third of the whites into the egg yolk mixture, then fold in the remaining whites, alternating with the ground nuts mixture. Combine everything gently but thoroughly.

Pour the batter into a well-greased 23-cm/9-in square cake tin, and bake for about 25 minutes or until the top is golden. Remove from the oven, and let the cake cool for about 10 minutes, then divide into squares and diamonds and pour over the cooled kumquat syrup. Serve the cake at room temperature.

The cake will keep for 2 days in an airtight container.

ORANGE SORBET

SHARBAT BI BORTUAN

MAKES ABOUT 1.25 L/2 PINTS

Everyday Arab *sharbat* is a very sweet flavoured syrup to be diluted and sipped rather than eaten. It is sold on street corners and served in homes. Adding egg white to lighten flavoured crushed ice was a refinement of the sultans to the sorbet – an invention of the Mogul emperors.

- *8 juicy oranges*
- *225 g/8 oz caster sugar*
- *30–45 ml/2–3 tbsp fresh lemon juice*
- *5–7.5 ml/1–1½ tsp orange flower water*
- *1 large egg white*
- *Fresh mint*

Thinly peel 2 of the oranges, trying to get as little pith as possible. In a food processor fitted with a metal blade, process the rind and sugar until the mixture is as well combined and mushy as possible. Transfer it into a saucepan and add 120 ml/4 fl oz water. Stir over high heat and bring the mixture to the boil, then lower the heat, cover and simmer for about 5 minutes. Cool, then chill until very cold.

Squeeze the oranges and measure out 1 l/1¾ pints of juice into a large bowl. Stir in the syrup, 30 ml/2 tbsp lemon juice, 5 ml/1 tsp orange flower water, and the egg white. Stir to combine, but do not beat.

Transfer the mixture to a freezer container and freeze for 5 hours or so, or until slushy. Scoop out the sorbet into the food processor, taste, and add extra lemon juice or orange flower water to taste. Blend until the ice crystals are broken down. Return to the container and freeze overnight. Serve in bowls garnished with sprigs of fresh mint.

YOGHURT AND ORANGE MOUSSE CAKE

SERVES 6

This is another "modern" dessert, with the flavours and spirit of the old Levant married to the health concerns of the new. It is also very simple to make.

- *3 large eggs, separated*
- *120 ml/4 fl oz milk*
- *250 ml/8 fl oz Greek-style yoghurt*
- *2.4 ml/½ tsp grated orange rind*
- *60 ml/4 tbsp fresh orange juice*
- *225 g/8 oz caster sugar*
- *25 g/1 oz plain flour*
- *5 ml/1 tsp vanilla essence*
- *Sweetened fruit yoghurt (optional)*

Preheat the oven to 180°C/350°F/Gas Mark 4.

In a bowl with an electric mixer, beat the separated egg yolks until thickened and pale. Add the milk and yoghurt, grated rind and orange juice, then beat in the 175 g/6 oz caster sugar, flour and vanilla until the mixture is smooth.

In a large bowl beat the egg whites on medium speed until they are foamy. Turn the speed up to high, and beat in the remaining 50 g/2 oz sugar until stiff peaks form.

Gently fold the yolk mixture into the whites until all is combined. Pour the batter into a 23-cm/9-in square cake tin.

Place the tin in a larger container and pour in boiling water until it comes halfway up the outer sides of the cake tin. Bake the cake in the oven for about 30 minutes or until it is golden. Serve with sweetened fruit yoghurt, if desired.

INDEX